LAND LAW

Toni Spencer

Series editors: Amy Sixsmith and David Sixsmith

First published in 2022 by Fink Publishing Ltd

British Library Cataloguing in Publication Data
A catalogue record for this book is available from the British Library
ISBN: 9781914213045

This book is also available in various ebook formats.
Ebook ISBN: 9781914213113

Multiple-choice question advisor: Mark Thomas
Cover and text design by BMLD (bmld.uk)
Production by River Editorial
Typeset by Westchester Publishing Services
Commissioning by R Taylor Publishing Services
Development Editing by Sonya Barker
Indexing by Terence Halliday

Fink Publishing Ltd
E-mail: hello@revise4law.co.uk
www.revise4law.co.uk

Contents

About the author

Toni Spencer works at the University of Sunderland as an academic tutor and supervising solicitor within the Student Law Clinic. She is module leader for both land law at undergraduate level and property and practice at postgraduate level and is actively involved in setting assessment questions to comply with the SQE specifications. Toni also holds the role of deputy programme leader for the LLB with specific focus on career and employability-related advice and guidance to all students across the LLB. She worked in private practice for nearly 20 years and many of the scenarios and additional guidance in this book are drawn from that professional experience.

Series editors

Amy Sixsmith is a senior lecturer in law and programme leader for LLB at the University of Sunderland, and a senior fellow of the Higher Education Academy.

David Sixsmith is a senior lecturer in law, programme leader for LPC at the University of Sunderland, and a senior fellow of the Higher Education Academy.

Introduction to Revise SQE

Welcome to *Revise SQE*, a new series of revision guides designed to help you in your preparation for, and achievement in, the Solicitors Qualifying Examination 1 (SQE1) assessment. SQE1 is designed to assess what the Solicitors Regulation Authority (SRA) refer to as 'functioning legal knowledge' (FLK); this is the legal knowledge and competencies required of a newly qualified solicitor in England and Wales. The SRA has chosen single best answer multiple-choice questions (MCQs) to test this knowledge, and *Revise SQE* is here to help.

PREPARING YOURSELF FOR SQE

The SQE is the new route to qualification for aspiring solicitors, introduced in September 2021 as one of the final stages towards qualification as a solicitor. The SQE consists of two parts:

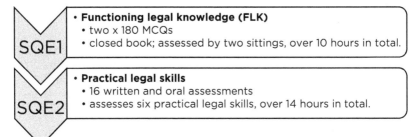

SQE1
- **Functioning legal knowledge (FLK)**
- two x 180 MCQs
- closed book; assessed by two sittings, over 10 hours in total.

SQE2
- **Practical legal skills**
- 16 written and oral assessments
- assesses six practical legal skills, over 14 hours in total.

In addition to the above, any candidate will have to undertake two years' qualifying work experience. More information on the SQE assessments can be found on the SRA website; this revision guide series will focus on FLK and preparation for SQE1.

It is important to note that the SQE can be perceived to be a 'harder' set of assessments than the Legal Practice Course (LPC). The reason for this, explained by the SRA, is that the LPC is designed to prepare candidates for 'day one' of their training contract; the SQE, on the other hand, is designed to prepare candidates for 'day one' of being a newly qualified solicitor. Indeed, the SRA has chosen the SQE1 assessment to be 'closed book' (ie without permitting use of any materials) on the basis that a newly qualified solicitor would know all of the information tested, without having to refer to books or other sources.

With that in mind, and a different style of assessments in place, it is understandable that many readers may feel nervous or wary of the SQE. This is especially so given that this style of assessment is likely to be different from what readers will have experienced before. In this *Introduction* and revision guide series, we hope to alleviate some of those concerns with guidance on preparing for the SQE assessment, tips on how to approach single best answer MCQs and expertly written guides to aid in your revision.

What does SQE1 entail?

SQE1 consists of two assessments, containing 180 single best answer MCQs each (360 MCQs in total). The table below breaks down what is featured in each of these assessments.

Assessment	Contents of assessment ('functioning legal knowledge')
FLK assessment 1	• Business law and practice • Dispute resolution • Contract • Tort • The legal system (the legal system of England and Wales and sources of law, constitutional and administrative law and European Union law and legal services)
FLK assessment 2	• Property practice • Wills and the administration of estates • Solicitors accounts • Land law • Trusts • Criminal law and practice

Please be aware that in addition to the above, ethics and professional conduct will be examined pervasively across the two assessments (ie it could crop up anywhere).

Each substantive topic is allocated a percentage of the assessment paper (eg 'legal services' will form 12–16% of the FLK1 assessment) and is broken down further into 'core principles'. Candidates are advised to read the SQE1 Assessment Specification in full (available on the SRA website). We have also provided a *Revise SQE checklist* to help you in your preparation and revision for SQE1 (see below).

HOW DO I PREPARE FOR SQE1?

Given the vastly different nature of SQE1 compared to anything you may have done previously, it can be quite daunting to consider how you could possibly prepare for 360 single best answer MCQs, spanning 11 different substantive topics (especially given that it is 'closed book'). The *Revise SQE FAQ* below, however, will set you off on the right path to success.

Revise SQE FAQ

Question	Answer
1. Where do I start?	We would advise that you begin by reviewing the assessment specification for SQE1. You need to identify what subject matter can be assessed under each substantive topic. For each topic, you should honestly ask yourself whether you would be prepared to answer an MCQ on that topic in SQE1.
	We have helped you in this process by providing a *Revise SQE checklist* on our website (revise4law. co.uk) that allows you to read the subject matter of each topic and identify where you consider your knowledge to be at any given time. We have also helpfully cross-referenced each topic to a chapter and page of our *Revise SQE* revision guides.
2. Do I need to know legal authorities, such as case law?	In the majority of circumstances, candidates are not required to know or use legal authorities. This includes statutory provisions, case law or procedural rules. Of course, candidates will need to be aware of legal principles deriving from common law and statute.
	There may be occasions, however, where the assessment specification does identify a legal authority (such as *Rylands v Fletcher* in tort law). In this case, candidates will be required to know the name of that case, the principles of that case and how to apply that case to the facts of an MCQ. These circumstances are clearly highlighted in the assessment specification and candidates are advised to ensure they engage with those legal authorities in full.

Revise SQE FAQ (Continued)

Question	Answer
3. Do I need to know the history behind a certain area of law?	While understanding the history and development of a certain area of law is beneficial, there is no requirement for you to know or prepare for any questions relating to the development of the law (eg in criminal law, candidates will not need to be aware of the development from objective to subjective recklessness). SQE1 will be testing a candidate's knowledge of the law as stated at the date of the assessment.
4. Do I need to be aware of academic opinion or proposed reforms to the law?	Candidates preparing for SQE1 do not need to focus on critical evaluation of the law, or proposed reforms to the law either.
5. How do I prepare for single best answer MCQs?	See our separate *Revise SQE* guide on preparing for single best answer MCQs below.

Where does *Revise SQE* come into it?

The *Revise SQE* series of revision guides is designed to aid your revision and consolidate your understanding; the series is not designed to replace your substantive learning of the SQE1 topics. We hope that this series will provide clarity as to assessment focus, useful tips for sitting SQE1 and act as a general revision aid.

There are also materials on our website to help you prepare and revise for the SQE1, such as a *Revise SQE checklist*. This *checklist* is designed to help you identify which substantive topics you feel confident about heading into the exam – see below for an example.

Revise SQE checklist

Land Law

SQE content	Corresponding chapter	*Revise SQE checklist*		
The nature and principles of land law • The distinction between real property and personal property	Chapter 1, pages 3–7	I do not know this subject and I am not ready for SQE1 ☐	I partially know this subject, but I am not ready for SQE1 ☐	I know this subject and I am ready for SQE1 ☐

Land Law (continued)

SQE content	Corresponding chapter	Revise SQE checklist		
The nature and principles of land law • Different ways in which land can be owned	Chapter 1, pages 7-10	I do not know this subject and I am not ready for SQE1 ☐	I partially know this subject, but I am not ready for SQE1 ☐	I know this subject and I am ready for SQE1 ☐
The nature and principles of land law • How to acquire and transfer legal estates	Chapter 1, page 10	I do not know this subject and I am not ready for SQE1 ☐	I partially know this subject, but I am not ready for SQE1 ☐	I know this subject and I am ready for SQE1 ☐
The nature and principles of land law • How to acquire and dispose of legal and equitable interests	Chapter 1, pages 10-12	I do not know this subject and I am not ready for SQE1 ☐	I partially know this subject, but I am not ready for SQE1 ☐	I know this subject and I am ready for SQE1 ☐

PREPARING FOR SINGLE BEST ANSWER MCQS

As discussed above, SQE1 will be a challenging assessment for all candidates. This is partly due to the quantity of information a candidate must be aware of in two separate sittings. In addition, however, an extra complexity is added due to the nature of the assessment itself: MCQs.

The SRA has identified that MCQs are the most appropriate way to test a candidate's knowledge and understanding of fundamental legal principles. While this may be the case, it is likely that many candidates have little, if any, experience of MCQs as part of their previous study. Even if a candidate does have experience of MCQs, SQE1 will feature a special form of MCQs known as 'single best answer' questions.

What are single best answer MCQs and what do they look like?

Single best answer MCQs are a specialised form of question, used extensively in other fields such as in training medical professionals. The idea behind single best answer MCQs is that the multitude of options available to a candidate may each bear merit, sharing commonalities and correct statements of law or principle, but only one option is absolutely correct (in the sense that it is the 'best' answer). In this regard, single best answer MCQs are different from traditional MCQs. A traditional MCQ will feature answers that are implausible in the sense that the distractors are 'obviously wrong'. Indeed, distractors in a traditional MCQ are often very dissimilar, resulting in a candidate being able to spot answers that are clearly wrong with greater ease.

In a well-constructed single best answer MCQ, on the other hand, each option should look equally attractive given their similarities and subtle differences. The skill of the candidate will be identifying which, out of the options provided, is the single best answer. This requires a much greater level of engagement with the question than a traditional MCQ would require; candidates must take the time to read the questions carefully in the exam.

For SQE1, single best answer MCQs will be structured as follows:

A woman is charged with battery, having thrown a rock towards another person intending to scare them. The rock hits the person in the head, causing no injury. The woman claims that she never intended that the rock hit the person, but the prosecution allege that the woman was reckless as to whether the rock would hit the other person.

The factual scenario. First, the candidate will be provided with a factual scenario that sets the scene for the question to be asked.

Which of the following is the most accurate statement regarding the test for recklessness in relation to a battery?

A. There must have been a risk that force would be applied by the rock, and that the reasonable person would have foreseen that risk and unjustifiably taken it.
B. There must have been a risk that force would be applied by the rock, and that the woman should have foreseen that risk and unjustifiably taken it.
C. There must have been a risk that force would be applied by the rock, and that the woman must have foreseen that risk and unjustifiably taken it.
D. There must have been a risk that force would be applied by the rock, and that both the woman and the reasonable person should have foreseen that risk and unjustifiably taken it.
E. There must have been a risk that force would be applied by the rock, but there is no requirement that the risk be foreseen.

The question. Next, the candidate will be provided with the question (known as the 'stem') that they must find the single best answer to.

The possible answers. Finally, the candidate will be provided with **five** possible answers. There is only one single best answer that must be chosen. The other answers, known as 'distractors', are not the 'best' answer available.

Now that you know what the MCQs will look like on SQE1, let us talk about how you may go about tackling an MCQ.

How do I tackle single best answer MCQs?

No exact art exists in terms of answering single best answer MCQs; your success depends on your subject knowledge and understanding of how that subject knowledge can be applied. Despite this, there are tips and tricks that may be helpful for you to consider when confronted with a single best answer MCQ.

1. Read the question twice	2. Understand the question being asked	3. If you know the answer outright	4. If not, employ a process of elimination	5. Take an educated and reasoned guess	6. Skip and come back to it later

1. Read the entire question at least twice

This sounds obvious but is so often overlooked. You are advised to read the entire question once, taking in all relevant pieces of information, understanding what the question is asking you and being aware of the options available. Once you have done that, read the entire question again and this time pay careful attention to the wording that is used.

- **In the factual scenario:** Does it use any words that stand out? Do any words used have legal bearing? What are you told and what are you not told?
- **In the stem:** What are you being asked? Are there certain words to look out for (eg 'should', 'must', 'will', 'shall')?
- **In the answers:** What are the differences between each option? Are they substantial differences or subtle differences? Do any differences turn on a word or a phrase?

You should be prepared to give each question at least two viewings to mitigate any misunderstandings or oversights.

2. Understand the question being asked

It is important first that you understand what the question is asking of you. The SRA has identified that the FLK assessments may consist of single best answer MCQs that, for example,

- require the candidate to simply identify a correct legal principle or rule
- require the candidate to not only identify the correct legal principle or rule, but also apply that principle or rule to the factual scenario
- provide the candidate with the correct legal principle or rule, but require the candidate to identify how it should be properly applied and/or the outcome of that proper application.

xii   Introduction to Revise SQE

By first identifying what the question is seeking you to do, you can then understand what the creators of that question are seeking to test and how to approach the answers available.

3. If you know the answer outright

You may feel as though a particular answer 'jumps out' at you, and that you are certain it is correct. It is very likely that the answer is correct. While you should be confident in your answers, do not allow your confidence (and perhaps overconfidence) to rush you into making a decision. Review all of your options one final time before you move on to the next question.

4. If you do not know the answer outright, employ a process of elimination

There may be situations in which the answer is not obvious from the outset. This may be due to the close similarities between different answers. Remember, it is the 'single best answer' that you are looking for. If you keep this in your mind, it will thereafter be easier to employ a process of elimination. Identify which answers you are sure are not correct (or not the 'best') and whittle down your options. Once you have only two options remaining, carefully scrutinise the wording used in both answers and look back to the question being asked. Identify what you consider to the be the best answer, in light of that question. Review your answer and move on to the next question.

5. Take an educated and reasoned guess

There may be circumstances, quite commonly, in which you do not know the answer to the question. In this circumstance, you should try as hard as possible to eliminate any distractors that you are positive are incorrect and then take an educated and reasoned guess based on the options available.

6. Skip and come back to it later

If time permits, you may think it appropriate to skip a question that you are unsure of and return to it before the end of the assessment. If you do so, we would advise

- that you make a note of what question you have skipped (for ease of navigation later on), and
- ensure you leave sufficient time for you to go back to that question before the end of the assessment.

The same advice is applicable to any question that you have answered but for which you remain unsure.

We hope that this brief guide will assist you in your preparation towards, and engagement with, single best answer MCQs.

GUIDED TOUR

Each chapter contains a number of features to help you revise, apply and test your knowledge.

Make sure you know   Each chapter begins with an overview of the main topics covered and why you need to understand them for the purpose of the SQE1 assessments.

SQE assessment advice   This identifies what you need to pay particular attention to in your revision as you work through the chapter.

What do you know already?   These questions help you to assess which topics you feel confident with and which topics you may need to spend more time on (and where to find them in the chapter).

Key term   Key terms are highlighted in bold where they first appear and defined in a separate box.

Exam warning   This feature offers advice on where it is possible to go wrong in the assessments.

Revision tip   Throughout the chapters are ideas to help you revise effectively and be best prepared for the assessment.

Summary   This handy box brings together key information in an easy to revise and remember form.

Practice example   These examples take a similar format to SQE-type questions and provide an opportunity to see how content might be applied to a scenario.

Procedural link   Where relevant, this element shows how a concept might apply to another procedural topic in the series.

Key point checklist   At the end of each chapter there is a bullet-point summary of its most important content.

Key terms and concepts   These are listed at the end of each chapter to help ensure you know, or can revise, terms and concepts you will need to be familiar with for the assessments.

SQE-style questions Five SQE-style questions on the chapter topic give you an opportunity to test your knowledge.

Answers to questions Check how you did with answers to both the quick knowledge test from the start of the chapter and the SQE questions at the end of the chapter.

Key cases, rules, statutes and instruments These list the key sources candidates need to be familiar with for the SQE assessment.

SQE1 TABLE OF LEGAL AUTHORITIES

The SQE1 Assessment Specification states the following in respect of legal authorities and their relevance to SQE1:

> On occasion in legal practice a case name or statutory provision, for example, is the term normally used to describe a legal principle or an area of law, or a rule or procedural step (eg *Rylands v Fletcher*, CPR Part 36, Section 25 notice). In such circumstances, candidates are required to know and be able to use such case names, statutory provisions etc. In all other circumstances candidates are not required to recall specific case names, or cite statutory or regulatory authorities.

This *SQE1 table of legal authorities* identifies the legal authorities you are required to know for the purpose of the SQE1 Functioning Legal Knowledge assessments for *Land Law*.

Legal authority	Corresponding *Revise SQE* chapter/pages
Trusts of Land and Appointment of Trustees Act 1996 s 14 s 15	Chapter 9: Co-ownership, pages 224 and 229 Chapter 9: Co-ownership, pages 224 and 225

TABLE OF CASES

TABLE OF STATUTES

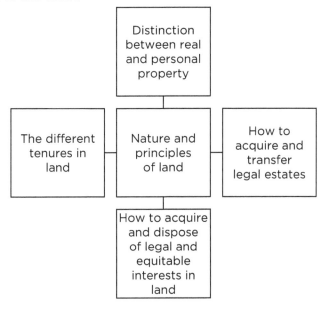

1

The nature and principles of land law

■ MAKE SURE YOU KNOW

This chapter will give you the necessary introduction to a wide range of basic principles that you must understand when considering a land law question, such as the differences between real and personal property, the different tenures in land, how to acquire and dispose of both legal and equitable interests and legal formalities required to create these interests.

There is no single explanation that we can give you which will explain exactly what 'land' is. It has a rich historical background and mix of common law, statute, policy and practice which is rarely seen in other legal disciplines. This chapter will start to explore some of these basic, but important, principles, which we will then cover in greater detail in the rest of this book.

■ SQE ASSESSMENT ADVICE

As you work through this chapter, remember to pay particular attention in your revision to:

- the distinction between real property and personal property/chattels
- different ways in which land can be owned
- how to acquire and transfer legal estates in land
- how to acquire and dispose of legal and equitable interests in land.

■ WHAT DO YOU KNOW ALREADY?

Try answering these questions before reading this chapter. If you find some difficult or cannot remember the answers, make a note to look more closely at that during your revision.

1) True or false? If you own a piece of land, you are entitled to take anything from that land, including gas, oil or water.

   [The definition of land, page 4]

2) You have been contacted by Ebony who has recently purchased a property in the Derwent Valley, which is surrounded by around two acres of woodland, all of which are contained within her title deeds. She is extremely concerned that a local photography company are flying over her property and she is aware they are taking pictures of her woodland and she wants to stop them. Which of the following is true in relation to her property law rights?

   a) As the woodland area is contained within Ebony's title deeds then she must inform the photography company that she does not give permission for them to fly over her land.

   b) When someone purchases land, they purchase everything 'reaching up to the very heavens'. Ebony can file a trespass claim against the photography company, which on this basis would be successful.

   c) There is nothing Ebony can do to stop the photography company taking pictures, but they have no right to sell them without her permission. Ebony will be entitled to any profits from any sales they make.

   d) Ebony's legal rights in the property will only extend to such a height as is necessary for her ordinary enjoyment of the land. Any aircraft flying above that height would not be trespassing on the land.

   e) Case law indicates that light aircraft flying at below 8,000ft will be classed as trespassing upon land. Ebony would need to obtain proof of the distance the photography company are flying at before she can assert her legal rights for trespass on her land.

[The definition of land: Airspace, page 5]

3) True or false? A fixture is anything which is part of the land and that could only be removed by demolishing or causing damage to the same.

[Fixtures and chattels, page 6]

4) James and Nicola have recently purchased a house together. They both contributed equally to the purchase price with a small contribution from a mortgage company. They are both named on the title deeds as the legal owners. What type of interest do they have in this property?

a) They both have a legal and equitable interest in the property.

b) They only have a legal interest as they are named on the title deeds.

c) They only have an equitable interest due to their equal contribution. The legal interest will be in the name of the mortgage company.

d) James will have a legal interest and Nicola will have an equitable interest.

e) Nicola will have a legal interest and James will have an equitable interest.

[The distinction between legal and equitable estates in land, page 8]

5) True or false? Restrictive covenants are always legal interests in land and permanently binding on future owners.

[Legal interests in land, page 10]

WHAT IS LAND?

There is no specific definition of what would encompass all 'land'. One definition has been provided by the Law of Property Act 1925 (LPA 1925) but before we consider this, a sensible starting point would be to break 'land' down into two separate components and consider the distinction between **real property** and **personal property.** The LPA 1925 does not provide clarity between these two types of property, but it does give us some important terms that we will consider throughout this chapter.

Key term: real property

Real property relates to all property which is generally considered to be immovable. So, this would be the land itself, but it also relates to any third-party rights in the land.

Key term: personal property

Personal property relates to anything which is not the 'real' property, so anything that could be moved.

The definition of land

We can now consider the partial definition of land that is provided for by the LPA 1925 which is as follows:

> 'Land' includes land of any tenure, and mines and minerals, whether or not held apart from the surface, buildings or parts of buildings ... and other corporeal hereditaments; ... and other incorporeal hereditaments, and an easement, right, privilege, or benefit in, over, or derived from land; ... and 'mines and minerals' include any strata or seam of minerals or substances in or under any land, and powers of working and getting the same ...; and 'hereditament' means any real property which on an intestacy occurring before the commencement of this Act might have devolved upon an heir.

So, as you can see, this could be quite confusing if read without a greater understanding of what 'land' can consist of. We shall break this down further as follows:

Land of any tenure

This means land which is freehold or leasehold. We will consider these in greater detail in **Chapter 4** and **Chapter 5**.

Mines and minerals

This is usually considered with an old Latin maxim translated to 'he who owns the land owns everything reaching up to the very heavens and down to the depths of the earth'; however, that does not give the owner unlimited rights and the courts and statute have set out some exceptions to this. Any coal, natural gas or oil beneath the land are deemed, by statute, to be the property of the Crown.

Revision tip

Fracking is something which is generating increasing concern with the public and as such, it is something that is now regularly raised with practitioners. This falls within a 'mine and mineral' so knowing who owns or has the rights to these is necessary to advise a client on these issues.

Airspace

This is another important consideration when looking at who owns the 'land' above the physical property. The courts have given clarification on the Latin maxim: 'he who owns the land owns everything reaching up to the very heavens and down to the depths of the earth', when considering cases relating to airspace and actions of trespass. **Practice example 1.1** gives an example of this.

Practice example 1.1

The owner of a large country estate has brought an action in trespass against a local company for flying over and taking photographs of his land. Does the airspace form part of the claimant's land?

These are the facts of *Bernstein v Skyviews* [1978] and the judge held that the owners' rights in the airspace above the land extended 'to such height as is necessary for the ordinary use and enjoyment of his land'. Above this height the landowner has no more rights than the public as aircraft flying at a normal height do not trespass upon land. The claimant lost the case.

Corporeal hereditaments

This is an old expression, but it simply means 'any real property having a physical form'. The hereditaments part simply means 'something that can be inherited'. Historically, for inheritance purposes it was essential for parties to establish the extent of real property. This would not only include the actual buildings on the land, but any other tangible items such as plants, animals, water and fixtures. Fixtures will be considered separately in this chapter.

Revision tip

When revising, keep in mind these distinctions:
• Plants: 'Land' will include any plants, trees and flowers that are attached to it and form part of it.

- Animals: Strangely, animals can form part of the 'land' but only if they are found dead on the land. Wild animals will not form part of the land while they are alive.
- Water: This is a rather complicated provision but, generally, any water which passes over or flows through the land will not form part of it. Landowners may have rights to take from the water, such as fishing rights, but they cannot extract great volumes of this water without prior permission from the appropriate authority.

Incorporeal hereditaments

These are the opposite to corporeal hereditaments and relate to anything that does not have a physical form, such as a right of way, rights of light or receiving rent from the land.

Fixtures and chattels

Fixtures and **chattels** are considered under the heading of 'corporal hereditaments', but they also have their own particular set of rules when determining which items fall into which category and so it is best to consider these separately. A good starting point is to understand what both terms mean.

Key term: fixture

Fixtures are objects that are considered to form part of the land and which will be transferred with that land automatically when it is sold, for example, a fitted kitchen unit. If the structure could only be removed by some form of demolition, then it is likely to be a fixture.

Key term: chattels

Chattels are personal possessions and have no connection or fixture with the land. Chattels will remain in possession of the owner and removed by them when they sell the land. For example, pictures on the walls.

Practice example 1.2 gives an example of how to differentiate between fixtures and chattels.

Practice example 1.2

The owner of a weaving mill purchased some looms to use with the mill (a loom is a device used to hold the threads under tension). They were attached to the stone floor by nails into wooden beams and could easily be removed. The owner failed to keep up mortgage repayments and the mill was repossessed. Were the looms fixtures (forming part of the land the mortgage company could repossess) or were the looms chattels and remained in possession of the owner?

These are the facts of *Holland v Hodgson* [1872] where the judge said that the test to determine whether an item was a fixture or a chattel was twofold. There needed to be consideration of:

a) the degree of annexation, which indicates that if detaching the object from the land would mean destroying it or causing significant damage, then it would be a fixture. If on the other hand it is simply resting on the land by virtue of its own weight, such as a wooden bungalow resting on concrete pillars, it would be considered a chattel.

b) the purpose of annexation, which does not consider the physical attachment, but considers why the item has been placed on the land. If there is an intention that it will be a permanent addition then it will be a fixture. If, however, it is there merely for convenience or for the purpose of creating a temporary improvement, then it will be a chattel.

The judge held that the looms were fixtures as they had been attached to the land.

DIFFERENT WAYS IN WHICH LAND CAN BE OWNED

Now that you have some understanding of what 'land' is, it is important to understand the ways in which someone can own land. An important point to make at this stage is that whilst we talk of 'owning' land, the reality is that the Crown are the absolute owners of all land in England and Wales. This is a clear relic of the historical aspects of land law as the Crown hold the tenure of all land and have granted licences of this land to individuals who then hold an **estate in land**, whilst others may acquire an interest in land.

By itself, the term **tenure** has very little impact on everyday land law practices, but the doctrine of this term remains an important one to be aware of. All historical 'tenures' were ended under the Tenures Abolition Act 1660, but the Crown continue to hold 'tenure' of land which means that should someone who has been granted an estate in land (now commonly known as the landowner), die without relatives or a Will, then the land would pass back to the Crown.

Key term: tenure

Tenure means 'to hold' and is the relationship between the landowner and the Crown.

Key term: estate in land

The term estate denotes how long a person will own that piece of land. There are only two types of legal estates available today and those are freehold (forever) and leasehold (for a fixed term). These will be explained in much greater detail in **Chapter 4** and **Chapter 5**.

THE DISTINCTION BETWEEN LEGAL AND EQUITABLE ESTATES IN LAND

The legal system for land law in England and Wales is separated into two distinctive parts, which are law, or **legal ownership**, and **equitable ownership**. Whilst land law would be far simpler if everyone had demonstrable legal rights in land, everyday life usually allows for third parties to have rights over land that belong to others, such as the right to pass over a neighbouring drive to access your own property.

As such, you will see that we have this dual system of law, and it is common to see land ownership divided into these two separate parts of law and equity. You will see many references to this dual system of law and equity throughout this book as it is a key concept of land law.

Key term: legal ownership

The legal ownership can be more commonly referred to as the formal and paper ownership, so the name on the title deeds. This will represent who has the legal right to sell or transfer that piece of land.

Key term: equitable ownership

This relates to any beneficial rights an individual or third party may have in the property, including the right to take money from it.

It is important to have a good understanding of these principles as whilst the legal ownership, or paper deeds, could show the property is owned by two different individuals, just looking at the deeds will tell you nothing about what could happen in equity, or what is fair between these legal owners. So, we also need to be aware of the equitable rights that they each have in this property.

Whilst both terms will be explored further in later chapters, **Practice example 1.3** gives an example of how these two principles work.

Practice example 1.3

James and Nicola are the legal owners of 29 Domino Lane. If they are both named on the title deeds and so have legal (or paper) ownership, then they will both have the right to sell or transfer the property. What would their ownership rights be if they were not both named on the title deeds but had both contributed towards the purchase price?

This can be a common occurrence and if, for example, Nicola purchased the property in her sole name and is the only party shown on the legal title (title deeds) but James contributed £50,000 to the purchase price then James would hold an equitable interest by way of a resulting trust, which is explained later in this chapter. Nicola, however, would be the only person entitled to sell or transfer the legal title of the property, unless James obtains an order from the court.

Figure 1.1 shows how legal and equitable owners can be different people.

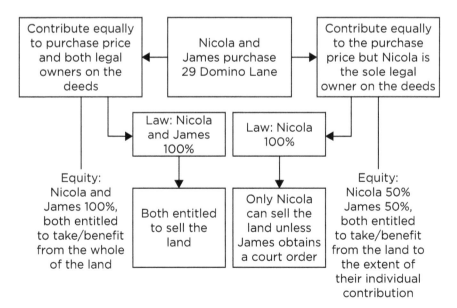

Figure 1.1: Understanding the difference between legal and equitable owners

To fully understand this principle, the next important consideration is exactly how individuals can acquire or transfer these legal estates, and how they can acquire legal and equitable interests in land.

HOW TO ACQUIRE AND TRANSFER LEGAL ESTATES IN LAND

There are now only the two legal estates that we have already mentioned, those being freehold and leasehold. Any other type of interest in land would be considered an equitable interest.

The most common way in which someone can acquire the legal estate in land would be by one individual purchasing land from another individual or inheritance under a Will, a transfer from parents to their children or by other means such as adverse possession, which is outside the scope of this revision guide.

Regardless of the way in which this legal estate can be acquired or transferred, it must be created by a **deed**.

Key term: deed

The Law of Property (Miscellaneous Provisions) Act 1989 (L(MP)A) sets out the formal requirements of a deed, which are:
- It is clear on the face of it that it is intended to be a deed.
- It is validly executed as a deed by the parties that are subject to it.

For a legal estate, this deed must also be registered with HM Land Registry to be valid, but we shall consider that in greater detail in **Chapter 4**.

HOW TO ACQUIRE AND DISPOSE OF LEGAL AND EQUITABLE INTERESTS IN LAND

Determining how to create a legal estate is somewhat straightforward, but there is a greater level of complexity when considering how to determine the validity of legal and equitable interests in land.

Legal interests in land

There are currently four legal interests in land. These are:
- easements (**Chapter 6**)
- legal mortgages (**Chapter 8**)

- a rentcharge, which is paid by the landowner of a freehold estate to a third party who normally has no other interest in the property. These have changed significantly since the introduction of the Rentcharges Act 1977, which looks to extinguish all rentcharges by 2037.
- rights of entry, this could be to a third party to legally take or resume possession of a property, such as if a tenant has breached the terms of a lease.

As with legal estates, the creation and disposal of legal interests in land is quite straightforward and there must be a deed which meets the requirements of LP(MP)A 1989. This would also need to be registered with HM Land Registry to hold its legal status.

Figure 1.2 sets out the two legal estates and the four legal interests which can currently be created.

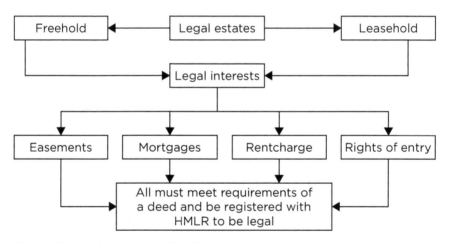

Figure 1.2: Legal estates and legal interests

The creation and disposal of equitable interests is more complicated.

Equitable interests in land

Should there be a failure to fully comply with the requirements to create a legal interest in land, such as not registering this with HM Land Registry, or if you have an interest which does not fall within the list shown in **Figure 1.2**, then that particular interest will take effect in equity only. The most common of these are:

- restrictive covenants
- beneficial interests under a trust
- estate contracts.

Restrictive covenants

These are considered in greater detail in **Chapter 7** and are rights over land by third parties who have no legal interest or ownership in the land. They are a promise by one landowner to another specifying certain things that they will not do upon the land. Some examples include:

• not keeping poultry or chickens on the land
• not altering the structure of the property without consent
• not using the property for any trade, business or other profession
• not keeping caravans or boats on the property.

Some of these covenants are a sign of the historical origins of how land was transferred, as the landowners would have tried to prevent certain competition within rural or farming communities; others are a sign of larger, modern developments where builders try to preserve the aesthetics of a housing estate and as such are part of a **building scheme**, which is a form of restrictive covenant.

Key term: building scheme
A restrictive covenant that forms part of a building scheme simply means all the properties will be subject to the same restrictive covenants. There is a specific system of enforcement that requires every property to be both servient land and also dominant land for the other properties. This allows for mutual enforcement of these restrictive covenants between the landowners. These are terms that we will explore in greater detail in **Chapter 7**.

Beneficial interests under a trust

Whilst it is common for a trust of land to be made expressly between the parties, by way of a deed, this interest can also arise as an equitable interest and can be imposed in law in three ways:

• constructive trusts
• resulting trusts
• proprietary estoppel.

They all have the same basic principle, in that it is a claim by someone who believes they have a beneficial interest in the property, and they wish to try to override the legal ownership. However, both constructive and resulting trust can be implied by the court due to the actions of the parties, and proprietary estoppel acts as a defence to prevent one party going back on a promise or from taking advantage of another's misbelief about their own legal rights in a piece of land.

- *Constructive trusts* arise where one party, who is not a legal owner of the property, contributes substantially to the repayment of the mortgage or pays for some substantial improvements to the property. **Practice example 1.4** gives an example of how this could arise.

Pactice example 1.4

Sarah purchases a property in her sole name for £275,000 and is the sole legal and equitable owner. Her mortgage repayments are £750 each month. After two years Georgina moves in with Sarah and starts contributing 50% to the mortgage payments each month; she also pays to renovate the house by contracting a single storey extension to the rear of the property and creating a large kitchen/diner/family room. The cost of this work amounts to around £50,000, which Georgina pays for using some inheritance. Sarah has spoken to Georgina about the property also being 'her house' and that everything is shared equally. Does Georgina have any interest in the property?

This is a very common scenario and there will be a plethora of case law which considers this exact issue. One of the most well-known cases is *Stack v Dowden* which is similar in nature to this example. Georgina does have grounds to show that a constructive trust has arisen due to the conduct of both her and Sarah. It is clear they both have a common intention, by their actions and words, to share the equitable ownership of the property and, as such, equity will assist Georgina here, in the event that Sarah tries to assert her legal rights in the property and tries to sell without making any contribution back to Georgina.

- *Resulting trusts* will only arise if one party has contributed to the purchase price of the property but is not a legal owner. **Practice example 1.4** shown above gives a very good example of how this equitable interest can arise.

Exam warning

You may receive a question asking which claim your client should make, either proprietary estoppel or constructive trusts, as those are the two which are very similar in nature. This is very difficult to answer without knowing the full context of the background between the parties, but generally, the preferred option for most parties would be a claim for a constructive trust, as the courts would usually look to provide relief to a claimant on the basis of what the parties actually intended; whereas with proprietary estoppel, the relief is generally considered as a minimum to show justice has been served, and there can often be ongoing and complex familial connections when considering any award.

- *Proprietary estoppel* works to prevent one party going back on a promise or from taking advantage of another's misbelief about their own legal rights in a piece of land. For example, a landowner may encourage a third party to spend money or effort on the land and makes assurances or promises to this person which makes them believe they will eventually gain some right or benefit to the landowner's property. So, the basic elements of a claim are that a promise was made, there was reliance upon that promise, and someone acted to their detriment. **Practice example 1.5** explains how this could arise.

Practice example 1.5

Stephen worked together on the family farm with his father, Roger, for most of his life. He was paid a wage as an adult which was more or less in line with the drawings taken by Roger at that time. The farm was owned by Roger and Stephen's uncle, Geoffrey, but there had been repeated promises made to Stephen that he would inherit Roger's share in the farm. A disagreement arose between Stephen and Roger which resulted in the partnership being dissolved, and Stephen made a claim in proprietary estoppel seeking that he would inherit Roger's share of the farm. What would the court consider in this case?

These are the very brief facts of *Moore v Moore* [2018]. Stephen was successful in his claim based on the promises made to him throughout his lifetime, with some rather complex financial settlements for the care of his father. Proprietary estoppel cases are heavily dominated by those within farming industries and can be very difficult for the courts to deal with.

Estate contracts

This is very much interlinked with conveyancing practice, which is outside the scope of this revision guide, but it is still necessary to be aware of this as a possible equitable interest.

An estate contract will arise at a very specific point in a conveyancing transaction, which is when the parties have exchanged contracts. This is the point at which the transaction becomes legally binding between the parties.

There can sometimes be a delay between this exchange stage and the actual completion taking place. During this time the new owner does not legally own the property but is still legally obligated to pay for the property on the completion date. This could be a precarious position for the new owner, as they could have paid a substantial amount of money at this point without having anything tangible to show for it. As equity aims to achieve fairness, the new owner obtains an interest in the land which is known as an estate contract. It simply confers the right to acquire that piece of land on the agreed completion date.

Figure 1.3 sets out the equitable interests.

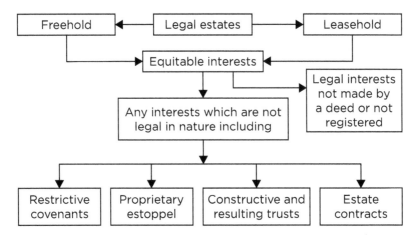

Figure 1.3: Equitable interests in land

Whilst the formation of these equitable interests can be quite subjective, it will be necessary to understand whether a new purchaser of that land would be bound by these interests. This will ultimately depend on whether the land in question is registered or unregistered, which we will consider in further detail in **Chapter 2** and **Chapter 3**.

■ KEY POINT CHECKLIST

This chapter has covered the following key knowledge points. You can use these to structure your revision around, making sure to recall the key details for each point, as covered in this chapter.

• What is land? This will include a consideration of what real property is, such as a house built on a piece of land which will be immovable, or only removed by being destroyed. This encompasses many different aspects, such as mines and minerals, airspace, corporeal hereditaments (tangible property) and incorporeal hereditaments (third party rights).

- You will need to understand the important distinction between fixtures, something that forms part of the land, and chattels, which can be removed from the land.
- Fixtures and chattels may also include consideration of the degree of annexation, so whether it is fixed to the land and only removable by being destroyed, or the purpose of annexation, so whether it is there simply as a temporary improvement.
- Remember that there are only two legal estates in land, those are freehold and leasehold.
- You will need to know the distinction between legal and equitable ownership. Legal ownership means the person who has the right to sell the property and equitable ownership means who has a right to take money from the land, such as the proceeds of sale.
- How to acquire and transfer legal estates in land, which is quite straightforward and any attempt to sell or transfer a legal estate must meet the requirements of a deed registered with HM Land Registry to be valid.
- How to acquire and dispose of legal and equitable interests in land, including knowing which interests are legal, such as easements and mortgages, and which are equitable, such as restrictive covenants and trusts.
- How to dispose of these legal and equitable interests in land will be considered in greater detail in **Chapter 2** and **Chapter 3**.

■ KEY TERMS AND CONCEPTS

- real property (**page 3**)
- personal property (**page 3**)
- fixtures (**page 6**)
- chattels (**page 6**)
- tenure (**page 7**)
- estate in land (**page 7**)
- legal ownership (**page 8**)
- equitable ownership (**page 8**)
- building scheme (**page 12**)

■ SQE1-STYLE QUESTIONS

QUESTION 1

A client, who owns a large area of undeveloped land, contacts a solicitor as he has discovered reserves of coal on his land. He asks the solicitor to send him a copy of his title deeds as he has been informed by a friend that he can sell the coal unless there is an agreement with the Coal Authority confirming that they own this.

Which of the following best represents the legal position?

A. For the Coal Authority to have any claim on this coal they need to have a specific legal agreement registered against the title deeds.

B. There is no requirement for a specific agreement from the Coal Authority, the client is entitled to sell any coal he finds and can dig to any level he likes as he owns everything above and below his land.

C. The client cannot extract this coal himself. He must ask the Coal Authority to do this for him. If they do they will cover all costs and give him 50% of the profits by way of compensation.

D. There is no requirement for a specific agreement from the Coal Authority, the client is entitled to sell any coal he finds but he can only dig to 300m below the surface level.

E. The client cannot extract this coal himself. All reserves of coal are owned by the Coal Authority who must grant licences for exploration and extraction of the same.

QUESTION 2

A client has recently purchased a property. Upon moving in, he has realised that the previous owners have removed all light fittings and light switches and replaced these with ones of far inferior quality. They have also removed a microwave that was integrated into the fitted kitchen unit and have caused damage to the surrounding cupboards when the microwave was removed. The client has spoken to the previous owner directly who has informed him that these items were their personal possessions, and they were told by their legal adviser to remove them.

How should the solicitor advise the client when considering these specific items?

A. Whether these items are classed as fixtures or chattels will depend upon the degree of annexation and the purpose of annexation. If there is any damage caused when removing these, they will be classed as fixtures; if, however, there is no damage, but the item was merely a temporary improvement then it will be a chattel. It is likely the client will only be able to make a claim for the microwave.

B. If the previous owner received advice from their legal adviser to remove these items then there is nothing the client can do, even if the advice is incorrect.

C. These items are all classed as chattels and the previous owner is entitled to remove them. There is nothing further the client can do.

D. These items are all classed as fixtures. The previous owner should not have removed them. The client must make a claim in the small claims court to recover any money lost in replacing these items.

E. Whether these items are classed as fixtures or chattels will entirely depend upon the degree of annexation only. If there is any damage caused when removing the items, they will all be classed as fixtures. The client will be able to make a claim for all items that have been removed.

QUESTION 3

A client has sought advice in respect to legal ownership of the property that she lives in with her husband. She has received a copy of the title deeds and it is only her husband who has legal ownership of the property. The client informs her solicitor that she was the one who paid the full purchase price for the property at the time and is now concerned that she will have to leave the property should her husband die before her and that she will have no way of getting her money back. She is now approaching her 80th birthday and wishes to make sure all her financial affairs are in order before she updates her Will.

Which of the following best represents the client's legal position?

A. The client is not shown as a legal owner on the title deeds and as such she does not have any legal ownership or entitlement to benefit from the property.

B. Regardless of whether the client is shown on the title deeds, she can clearly show that she has legal ownership in the property as she has paid for the purchase of the property in full. The property will automatically transfer to her on her husband's death.

C. As she has contributed to the purchase price the client will hold an interest in the property. Her husband owns the whole of the legal ownership but holds this on trust for the client by way of a resulting trust. The client is entitled to 100% of the equity if the property is sold.

D. As she has contributed to the purchase price, the client will hold an interest in the property. However, as she is married this will be limited to a 50% interest. If the client's husband dies, the property will be sold, and she will receive 50% of the equity.

E. As she has contributed to the purchase price, the client will hold an interest in the property. The client's husband owns the whole of the legal ownership but holds this on trust for her by way of a constructive trust. The client is entitled to 100% of the equity if the property is sold.

QUESTION 4

A Building Society has sought legal advice on their interest in 84 Lower Mast Farm, upon which they were granted a mortgage five years ago. The legal owners have defaulted on the mortgage and the Building Society wish to seek possession of the property. They have obtained a copy of the title deeds which do not show their legal interest. It has transpired that whilst the Deed was correctly executed, it was never registered with HM Land Registry.

Which of the following best represents the legal position of the Building Society?

A. For a legal interest in land to be valid, there must be a valid deed and it must be executed. If this has happened then there is nothing for the Building Society to worry about and their legal interest is protected.

B. For a mortgage to be a valid legal interest, there must be a valid deed, it must be executed and it must also be registered with HM Land Registry to take effect as a legal interest. If it has not been registered in this way then the mortgage will be an equitable one only. The Building Society can still assert their rights in full if they register a notice against the title deeds.

C. For a mortgage to be a legal interest it must be executed and it must also be registered with HM Land Registry to take effect as a legal interest. If it has not been registered in this way then the Building Society have no way of enforcing any of their rights.

D. As the Building Society has contributed towards the purchase price, they can clearly demonstrate that they have an equitable interest in the land by way of a constructive trust.

E. For a mortgage to be a valid legal interest, there must be a valid deed and it must be executed and they must register a restriction in the property register of the title deeds. If these have been satisfied then there is nothing for the Building Society to worry about and their legal interest is protected.

QUESTION 5

A client has sought advice on the validity of an agreement made with a neighbour over the purchase of a small strip of the neighbouring land. This was a verbal agreement between them, and the neighbour told the client that the land would be left to him in his Will. The neighbour has recently died and the client has been made aware that there is no Will and the entire neighbouring estate, including the strip of land promised to him, has been inherited by the neighbour's family. They are now refusing to uphold the verbal agreement.

Does the client have any demonstrable interest in the neighbouring land?

A. As the neighbour had verbally promised this land to the client there was no need for a deed. As long as the parties were in agreement with the transaction then it will be valid and the client can enforce this agreement against the neighbour's family.

B. As the neighbour had verbally promised this land to the client then there was no need for a deed and the client can rely on the doctrine of promissory estoppel to enforce this agreement against the neighbour's family.

C. As the neighbour has verbally promised this land to the client then there would be no legal estate demonstrated unless a deed has been signed and it has been registered with HM Land Registry. That would have then transferred the land from the legal ownership of the neighbour to the client. As this has not happened and the land has not been left in a Will then the client will have no claim against the neighbouring estate.

D. As the neighbour has verbally promised this land to the client then this would be a legal interest in the land by way of right of entry. The client has the right to use the land for as long as he wishes in accordance with the agreement made.

E. As the neighbour has verbally promised this land to the client then this would be an equitable right by way of a constructive trust. The client has the right to use the land for as long as he wishes in accordance with the agreement made.

◼ ANSWERS TO QUESTIONS

Answers to 'What do you know already?' questions at the start of the chapter

1) The correct answer was false. Mines and minerals have been deemed by statute to be the property of the Crown. Other corporeal hereditaments, such as plants and animals can form part of the land, except for water, but landowners can be granted rights to take from the water.

2) The correct answer was D. Airspace is only included in the land to such a height as is necessary for the ordinary use and enjoyment of the land. Whilst that can be subjecting in nature, it is not expected that any landowner will need to use airspace to the height that aircraft will use and as such it is not considered trespass.

3) The correct answer was true. A general rule is that if you need to destroy or damage an item to remove the same then it would be considered a fixture and form part of the land. Where there is any ambiguity over this then the courts would look at the degree and purpose of annexation to determine whether something is a fixture or chattel.

4) The correct answer was A. They are both named on the title deeds and so both hold the legal estate in the land. They also both contributed equally to the purchase price and as such they are both entitled to the equity from the land and so hold the equitable interest together.

5) The correct answer was false. Restrictive covenants are only ever going to be equitable interests in land. They may be permanently binding on future owners, but that does not in itself make it a legal interest.

Answers to end-of-chapter SQE1-style questions

Question 1:
  The correct answer was E. This is because despite 'mines and minerals' being included within the statutory definition of land, all mines were privatised in 1994 and as such, statute now confirms that reserves of coal will not belong to individual landowners. Options A–D are all incorrect as they suggest that the client can extract the coal, either with permission or in the absence of any legal agreement registered against the title deeds.

Question 2:
  The correct answer was A. This is because whether an item is a fixture or a chattel is usually fairly straightforward, but where there

is any ambiguity you need to consider the degree of annexation and the purpose of annexation. Here, the microwave was part of a fitted kitchen and damage has been caused when removing it, meaning it is a fixture. The light fittings and switches, however, are unlikely to have caused damage when being removed and so the purpose of annexation would be considered; here it would seem obvious that they were fitted to create a temporary improvement and so would be a chattel. Option B is incorrect as if there has been incorrect legal advice given then the client may well have a private action against that solicitor and so it is incorrect to say there is nothing he can do. Options C, D and E are incorrect as they do not consider that one of the items is a fixture and the other is a chattel.

Question 3:

The correct answer was C. This is because this is a clear example of a trust, which provides an equitable right to the party who does not have legal ownership of the property. Option A is incorrect as whilst it is true that the client does not have legal ownership, this also states that she has no entitlement to benefit from the property, which is incorrect. Option B is incorrect as legal ownership of property does not transfer automatically. There must always be a deed registered with HM Land Registry. Option D is incorrect as this states that the client's interest is limited to 50%; as she contributed 100% of the purchase price then it is not limited to 50% simply due to their marriage. Option E is incorrect as this refers to a constructive trust. The distinction between the resulting and constructive trust is that this was a direct contribution to the purchase price, which makes this a resulting trust.

Question 4:

The correct answer was B. This is because this is a clear example of the principles of fairness that equity provides. It would be unjust for the mortgagee to lose their investment due to no fault of their own. The requirements have not been met for this to be a legal mortgage and so it will automatically fall to an equitable interest. They do need to register a notice against the title deeds, which is considered further in Chapters 2 and 8. Options A and E are incorrect as legal interests are only valid if they are made by a deed and registered. Option C is incorrect as it states that the Building Society have no way of enforcing their rights; however, if they register a notice against the title deed, they can enforce their rights. Option D is incorrect as the grant of a mortgage does not confer an equitable interest upon a mortgage lender by way of a constructive trust.

Question 5:

The correct answer was C. This is because there is no legal estate here as there is no deed and it has not been registered. The neighbour could have left the land in a Will as landowners are entitled to transfer land in this way, but as he has not done this then the rules of intestacy will apply, and the client has no claim on the estate on a verbal promise. Option A would not be the best answer since it is notoriously difficult to demonstrate a valid verbal agreement. Option B is incorrect as you do not have enough information to demonstrate that there is promissory estoppel here, which requires a person to act to their detriment on the promise of another. We do not know that the client has acted to his detriment. Option D is incorrect as rights of entry are legal interests and so must be made by a deed. Option E is incorrect as you would need to demonstrate that the client has made a significant contribution to the upkeep or other payment on the land. You do not have this information to be able to select this as an answer.

■ KEY CASES, RULES, STATUTES AND INSTRUMENTS

The SQE1 Assessment Specification does not require you to know any case names, or statutory materials, for the topic of land law. Despite this, you may find it useful to become familiar with these statutes:

Law of Property Act 1925

Law of Property (Miscellaneous Provisions) Act 1989.

2

Unregistered land

We have separated out registered and unregistered land as there are some fundamental differences between the two, especially when considering very specific rules relating to how things such as the third-party interests, discussed in **Chapter 1**, are enforceable upon the landowner.

Unregistered land does not mean that there is no legal ownership of that land, simply that the ownership has not been registered (recorded) at HM Land Registry. HM Land Registry estimates that around 13% of land in England and Wales remains unregistered but the Government aims to achieve as close to 100% comprehensive registration by 2030. Whilst the principles relating to unregistered land are becoming less important, as there is less exposure to it, there is still land that remains unregistered so it is still important to be aware of the rules relating to it.

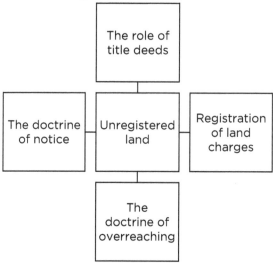

■ SQE ASSESSMENT ADVICE

As you work through this chapter, remember to pay particular attention in your revision to:
- what role title deeds have in unregistered land
- the system of land registration known as land charges
- how to protect third-party interests in unregistered land
- the continuing role of the doctrine of notice
- the doctrine of overreaching.

■ WHAT DO YOU KNOW ALREADY?

Try answering these questions before reading this chapter. If you find some difficult or cannot remember the answers, make a note to look more closely at that subtopic during your revision.

1) True or false? In unregistered land the owner must produce paper title deeds to prove their ownership and those deeds must date back at least 25 years?

    [What is unregistered land?, page 26]

2) Geraldine has lived and worked on the family farm all her life. Her parents have recently died and she is trying to register the land for the first time with HM Land Registry. She cannot find the title deeds and believes they were lost in a fire some 40 years ago. She applies for registration. What class of title is she likely to be granted?

    a) absolute title

    b) possessory title

    c) qualified title

    d) good leasehold

    e) good freehold

    [The role and importance of title deeds, page 27]

3) Which of the following is NOT a legal right which would automatically be binding on a purchaser of unregistered land?

    a) puisne mortgages

    b) easements

    c) mortgages

    d) rentcharges

    e) leases

    [The system of land registration known as land charges: Legal rights, page 30]

4) Andre is purchasing an unregistered house. A search of the Land Charges Register is undertaken and this reveals a Class D (ii) entry. What does this mean?

   a) The property is subject to a legal easement and if Andre purchases the property he will be bound by it as he has knowledge of it.

   b) The property is subject to an estate contract. This is automatically binding on any future purchasers.

   c) The property is subject to a restrictive covenant but as it has been revealed on the Land Charges Register, Andre will not be bound by it and it can be ignored.

   d) Andre must pay the purchase money over to two trustees to overreach this so that he is not bound by it.

   e) The property is subject to a restrictive covenant and it is binding as an equitable interest as it has been registered. It would be binding even if Andre had no knowledge of it.

   [The system of land registration known as land charges: Equitable rights, page 30]

5) Which of the following will NOT be binding on a purchaser in good faith for money or money's worth of a legal interest in unregistered land?

   a) all pre-existing legal interests except for an unregistered puisne mortgage

   b) an unregistered puisne mortgage where the proceeds of sale were paid to a single vendor

   c) an estate contract that has been protected as a C(iv) land charge

   d) an equitable easement created in 1926 and protected as a D(iii) land charge

   e) a beneficial interest of which the purchaser has notice where the proceeds of sale were paid to a single trustee

   [Methods to protect and enforce third-party interests, page 33]

WHAT IS UNREGISTERED LAND?

There are two systems of land ownership, those being unregistered and registered. These run in parallel with each other but are entirely separate and do not overlap. Unregistered land is land that has not been recorded with HM Land Registry and, as there is no central register of this land, ownership of it must be evidenced by the owner producing their **title deeds** for the land and showing they have a good **root of title** to prove that ownership.

A good root of title document must show the ownership of the full legal title and equitable interests in the land, it must contain a recognisable description of the property. It should not cast any doubt on the legitimacy of the title. It is highly likely there will then be other title deeds to support this root of title document.

Key term: title deeds

This can be a single or a series of documents which the landowner can use to prove their ownership of the land. This will ensure that no one can dispute this ownership claim.

Key term: root of title

A root of title is a deed which must show an unbroken chain of ownership and date back at least 15 years from the time the landowner is trying to dispose of the land.

The role and importance of title deeds

If the landowner does not have any title deeds or is unable to show a good root of title then that does not mean they can never register the land with HM Land Registry. However, it may affect the class of title they are granted. They may also be at risk of another person appearing with a deed to the land that shows that they have good root of title and therefore a better claim to the land. In such circumstances, that person could be awarded a better class of title to the land than the landowner themselves. **Practice example 2.1** explains how this may occur.

Practice example 2.1

Geraldine and her parents have lived on the family farm their whole lives. Geraldine's parents have recently died and she is now trying to register the title deeds with HM Land Registry. She believed the farm had been transferred to her in the 1980s by way of a transfer deed, but she cannot find this deed and the farmland therefore remains unregistered. Her parents did not leave the farm to her in their Wills as they believed she was already the owner. Their Will leaves all their assets to her brother, with whom she does not get on. Can Geraldine make an application to HM Land Registry to register the property in her name?

There are several different ways in which we could unpick this scenario, but the simple answer is yes, she can. Whether she will be successful will depend on the evidence she can produce to prove

her ownership. Without the deed transferring the land to her she may find this difficult but if successful she is likely to be granted a possessory title only. Her brother may be able to demonstrate that he has better proof of title by producing the Will which transfers all assets to him, which would include the farm.

Practice example 2.1 may start to illustrate some of the difficulties that can arise if someone does not have the paper title deeds to land when they apply to register the land (**Chapter 3** considers how and when registration must take place). **Table 2.1** sets out the different classes of ownership HM Land Registry will grant depending on the evidence provided in support of the proof of ownership; these are shown in hierarchy of the best possible title that can be granted.

Table 2.1: Classes of title granted by HM Land Registry

Absolute title	The best class of title that can be granted over land and it is a guarantee to the landowner against any other person trying to claim a legal interest in the land.
Possessory title	This would arise where the landowner cannot produce sufficient documentary evidence to prove their ownership.
Qualified title	This will be granted if there is a specific defect in the title and will be stated on the register.
Good leasehold	This is likely to occur if someone tries to register their leasehold interest for the first time, but the freehold estate has not yet been registered. This will be explored in greater detail in **Chapter 5**.

Taking **Practice example 2.1**, if Geraldine is successful in her application for registration, but is only granted a possessory title, she can apply to upgrade her class of title to an absolute title if she finds the missing deed or if she stays in possession of the land for at least 12 years without her brother, or any other person claiming they have a better class of title to the land.

Exam warning

Remember, if dealing with this type of question in the exam then the class of title is important as it may affect the future saleability of a property, especially in circumstances where there is a chance that someone else could produce evidence to demonstrate that they are the legal owners.

THE SYSTEM OF LAND REGISTRATION KNOWN AS LAND CHARGES

The introduction of the Law of Property Act 1925 allowed for two different systems of registration. The first, as mentioned above, is permanent registration of land on a central register, which we will explore in greater detail in **Chapter 3**. The second system relates to unregistered land only and was designed to be a less permanent system, ceasing once all land was registered.

This alternative system is called the Land Charges Register. It is important to note here that the Land Charges Register does not allow for registration of the land itself. The land remains unregistered. However, the Land Charges Register does allow for certain interests belonging to third parties to be registered against the name of the landowner. This was a way of ensuring that these rights were protected in the event that the owner subsequently sold the property without notifying the person with the benefit of the particular interest. If an interest is registered as a land charge, we refer to this as being 'binding on a future purchaser'. This means that a purchaser of the land will be subject to the interest whether they knew about it or not. **Practice example 2.2** explains this in more detail.

Practice example 2.2

Castor has owned a parcel of land since 1950. It remains unregistered but he entered into a freehold covenant with a neighbour in 1955 ensuring he maintained and painted the boundary fences every five years. Castor is now selling the parcel of land. Will the new purchaser be bound by this covenant?

As you will see as you work through this chapter, this is an example of a right which MUST be registered on the Land Charges Register in order to bind a purchaser. If it is registered then once registration has taken place it will automatically transfer over to the permanent land registration system and be recorded against the title deeds for that property, meaning it will bind a future purchaser, demonstrating this hybrid or interim system of recording rights.

Legal and equitable rights

Legal rights in unregistered land are binding under the principle that legal rights bind the world. Equitable rights in unregistered land will bind anyone if they are registered on the Land Charges Register or will bind anyone *except* a purchaser who pays money for the estate and has no notice of the third-party right. We shall consider both type of rights in turn.

Legal rights

By the very nature of title deeds, there may already be legal rights contained within unregistered title deeds, such as easements to third parties. If unregistered land is sold, transferred or if there is any other registrable disposition (**Chapter 3** explains this in greater detail), then upon completing that registration process, those legal rights will continue to be included within the title deeds. In effect, these legal rights are indestructible and 'bind the world'. It will bind anyone else who ever comes into ownership of that land since it is contained in the title deeds. Those legal rights which must be registered to be binding are set out in **Chapter 1**.

There is one exception to this with unregistered land and that is any **puisne mortgages**, which are registrable as a land charge and will be binding on a future landowner if registered against the name of the landowner on the Land Charges Register.

Key term: puisne mortgage

A puisne mortgage is a second or subsequent mortgage of unregistered land and where the title deeds are retained by the first mortgagee. Registration of these mortgages as a land charge is necessary to protect the mortgagee's legal interest as they would not be able to produce the title deeds to prove their legal ownership.

Equitable rights

Equitable rights are split into those that can be registered as a land charge and those that are **overriding**.

Key term: overriding

These are rights which 'override' a registrable disposition and will bind any future landowner even if they are not included on the title deeds. The only way a new landowner can discover the existence of any overriding interests is by making enquiries and visiting the property, which we will consider later in this chapter.

The Land Charges Act 1972 sets out very clear categories of the equitable rights that MUST be registered as a land charge to be binding on a new landowner. Equitable rights that cannot be registered as a land charge, or where there is a failure to register for any reason, would be governed by the doctrine of notice. **Table 2.2** lists the six categories of land charges.

Table 2.2: Categories of land charges

Class A	Financial charges created by statute, such as rent charged by a landlord. An application must be made to secure the charge.
Class B	Financial charges created by statute but no application is needed and they are applied automatically. An example would be the costs of legal aid.
Class C	i) A puisne mortgage; referred to earlier in this chapter. ii) A limited owners charge; usually arises where someone who has ownership under a settlement has spent money on the property. iii) A general equitable charge. iv) An estate contract, which we considered in **Chapter 1**.
Class D	i) An inland revenue charge; usually in relation to unpaid inheritance tax. ii) A restrictive covenant; this is the most common land charge that you are likely to see in unregistered land iii) An equitable easement.
Class E	Annuities created before 1st January 1926 and not registered on the annuities register. It is becoming increasingly unlikely that you will see these.
Class F	Charges created by the Family Law Act 1996, such as statutory home rights of occupation in the matrimonial/ civil partnership home.

Revision tip

It is important to note that those equitable rights that can be registered as a land charge relate only to those that have been created because of the LPA 1925; any equitable rights created prior to the introduction of this legislation (1st January 1926) will only be binding if the purchaser had prior notice of it.

The effect of registering these equitable interests against the name of the landowner on the central Land Charges Register is that the interest in question will be binding on any future owner of the land, whether they check the Land Charges Register before they purchase the land or not. If the interest was not registered then it will not be binding unless the purchaser falls outside the criteria set out in the doctrine of notice. The doctrine of notice is explained fully on page 33. **Practice example 2.3** gives an example of this.

Practice example 2.3

Walter is the legal owner of unregistered land, and he granted an option to purchase this land to his son, Geoffrey. This is an estate contract and so should be registered at the central Land Charges Register as a C(iv) land charge to be binding upon any future landowner. Geoffrey failed to register the estate contract as a land charge against Walter's name. Walter and Geoffrey fell out and Walter sold the land to his wife (Geoffrey's mother) for £500, grossly under the value of the land which is around £40,000. This is an attempt to defeat the unregistered option and Geoffrey wishes to seek a declaration that the option is still binding and to enforce the contract. What is the likely outcome?

These are the facts of *Midland Bank v Green* [1981] where the Land Charges Act 1972 was considered by the court and judged to be very clear and definite on the position of unregistered land charges, namely that an unregistered estate contract is void unless it is registered as a land charge or unless it has been sold or gifted to someone for no payment in return. It was not registered and despite it being below market value, Geoffrey's mother paid money for the land, so the estate contract was not binding against her.

Figure 2.1 shows a summary of the main points to consider when looking at third-party rights in unregistered land.

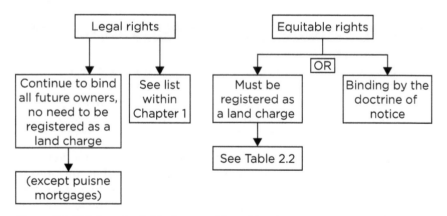

Figure 2.1: Third-party rights in unregistered land

METHODS TO PROTECT AND ENFORCE THIRD-PARTY INTERESTS

There are clear advantages of third parties being able to demonstrate their interests in land and as we have seen, there are certain circumstances where these interests must be registered to be enforceable. Where the Land Charges Act does not allow for a third-party interest to be registered as a land charge (so any equitable right that does not fall within **Table 2.2**), whether the interest is binding or not depends on whether the purchaser is what is referred to as a 'bona fide purchaser for value of the legal estate without notice'. This is called the doctrine of notice.

The doctrine of notice

The case of *Pilcher v Rawlins* [1872] established four specific elements which still need to be satisfied to demonstrate the doctrine of notice today. This is known as the bona fide purchaser of the legal estate for value without notice. To understand this properly it is worth breaking the phrase down in to these four elements:

- Bona fide is another Latin phrase still used in property law and simply means 'in good faith' – ie 'honestly' and without any fraudulent intention.
- Purchaser of the legal estate means that there must be a purchase of either a freehold or leasehold estate in land. It will not apply to anyone who purchases an equitable interest in land and will also not apply to someone who inherits or is gifted the land as they do not meet the strict definition of 'purchaser'. It does however extend to mortgagees and lessees.
- For value means that valuable consideration must be made by the purchaser, which includes payment below the market value of the land. This again excludes those that receive property by way of inheritance or gift as they have not made any valuable consideration for the land.
- Without notice is the element that clearly embraces the fairness and conscience principles of equity. Simply put, if someone knows of the equitable interest and still proceeds with the purchase then they should be bound by it; if they are not aware of it then they should not be bound by it.

'Notice' can take one of three forms.

Actual notice

This simply means the purchaser is aware of the equitable interest. It does not really matter how they come to receive notice, but things like casual conversations or vague rumours will not be actual notice.

Constructive notice

This puts a high burden of inspection on purchasers as they will be deemed to have constructive notice of any equitable right which they should have known about had they made reasonable enquiries by inspecting the title deeds and inspecting the land. Failure to do this means they would be bound by any equitable interests that these inspections and enquiries would have revealed.

Imputed notice

This ultimately extends the constructive notice to any agent that is instructed by the purchaser, for example, a solicitor instructed to deal with the purchase of land. If there is anything that they know or would have known about had they made reasonable enquiries of the title deeds and the land, this will be ascribed to the purchaser and binding on them.

Exam warning

It is important to note that 'agent' extends to all forms of agent, so not just solicitors, and will be any third party who is instructed to carry out any of the purchase enquiries on behalf of the purchaser. Most commonly these will be solicitors and surveyors, but just be mindful of this if you receive a question on this issue.

Practice example 2.4 shows how these notice provisions may work.

Practice example 2.4

Mr Tizard owned the family home in his own name and Mrs Tizard held an equitable interest in the property. Their marriage broke down and Mrs Tizard stopped living in the family home but would sleep there when Mr Tizard was away. She also kept her belongings at the home and would be there every morning and evening to care for the children. Mr Tizard arranged for a loan to be secured against the house by way of a mortgage. He informed the bank that he was single and an agent for the bank visited the property for valuation purposes. Mr Tizard informed him that his wife had moved out. The agent saw evidence of the children's occupation but not Mrs Tizard. Mr Tizard defaulted on the loan and the bank sought possession of the property. Would Mrs Tizard be able to defend this application on the basis that the bank had received constructive notice of her interest in the property?

These are the facts from the very well-known case of *Kingsnorth Finance Co v Tizard* [1986] where the court held that the bank did have constructive notice of Mrs Tizard's interest and so they could only enforce their rights against Mr Tizard's share of the equitable interest. The fact that Mr Tizard had described himself as single and made references to being separated from his wife, and there was evidence of the children in the house, should have alerted the bank to make more enquiries, and if they had, then they would probably have revealed Mrs Tizard's existence and equitable interest. It was also clear that Mr Tizard had arranged the inspection to take place at a time when he knew Mrs Tizard would not be present.

The doctrine of overreaching

A final consideration in unregistered land is how the doctrine of **overreaching** may apply, which can be seen as a defence mechanism to protect purchasers and allow them to take the property free of any unknown equitable interests.

The basic principle of a third-party right in property is that these rights are held within that specific parcel of land; therefore, against anyone who legally owns that parcel of land. Taking **Practice example 2.4**, Mrs Tizard had an equitable interest in the property. Overreaching is the principle whereby the equitable interest is taken out of the specific parcel of land and placed with an individual instead. The effect of this is that the claim in relation to the equitable interest transfers to the individual rather than being against the land. Applying this to the example above, if Mrs Tizard's equitable interest had been overreached, she would have a claim against Mr Tizard for her equitable interest rather than against the land itself or the future owner of that land.

Key term: overreaching

Overreaching is a mechanism to protect an innocent purchaser from being bound by an unknown equitable interest in land. It works by removing the interest from the land when it is sold and instead placing it with the sale proceeds or whoever the sale proceeds are paid to. This means that the purchaser is not bound by the interest but equally the interest holder does not lose their right because of the land being sold.

Overreaching applies to those equitable interests which are non-commercial or cannot be registered as a land charge (see **Table 2.2** on page 31). Principally, for land law these equitable interests will relate to those interests that have been created under a **trust of land**.

Key term: trust of land
An agreement, either in writing or by actions between the parties, in which the formal legal ownership of the land is separated from the underlying ownership, or the equitable ownership. This is considered in detail in **Chapter 1**.

For the doctrine of overreaching to be effective, the following criteria must be met:

- there must be an interest which is capable of being overreached, such as payment towards the purchase price by someone who is not a legal owner
- there must be a conveyance to a purchaser of a legal estate and
- that purchaser must pay the purchase money to at least two trustees or a trust corporation.

This means that overriding interests will not be available as a defence mechanism to a purchaser who pays the purchase money over to a single landowner/trustee. **Practice example 2.5** shows an example of this doctrine.

Practice example 2.5
Zendaya and Iman are purchasing 87 Wheeler Avenue from Mr Clancy. They are unaware that a friend of Mr Clancy, Simone, holds an equitable interest in the property due to her contribution to the purchase price, which is not registrable as a land charge. Would Zendaya and Iman purchase the property subject to this unregistered and unknown third-party interest?
This is different from Practice example 2.1 as that was a right which MUST have been registered as a land charge. Here, this is a right which does not fall within those categories of rights that are capable of being registered and so would entirely depend on whether the purchase money had been paid to two trustees. If it has, then the interest can be displaced (overreached) and removed from the land into the money itself, meaning Zendaya and Iman would purchase the property free of this interest. Simone would no longer have a claim for her interest in the property, but rather against the trustees, so whoever the purchase money has been paid to.

In **Practice example 2.5**, we are aware that there is only one legal owner of the land. If there have been two legal owners then this would not be a problem and overreaching automatically occurs where purchase money is paid over to two legal owners. However, in this scenario, if another trustee is not appointed and the money paid over to Mr Clancy alone, then any purchaser may be bound by Simone's third-party interest. This is *unless* they can demonstrate that they have the protection of the doctrine of notice, where they will have to show that they are a *bona fide purchaser for value without notice*. They would be required to make the reasonable enquiries mentioned within the explanation of **constructive notice**, earlier in this chapter.

Exam warning

Due to the uncertainty of third-party interests in unregistered land, it is always advisable that when dealing with the sale of unregistered land by a sole legal owner, a second trustee is appointed, and the purchase money paid to these two trustees. This will ensure that any unknown and unregistered equitable interests are overreached and allows the purchasers to take the property free of those interests.

Figure 2.2 shows how you would work your way through a question dealing with equitable interests in unregistered land.

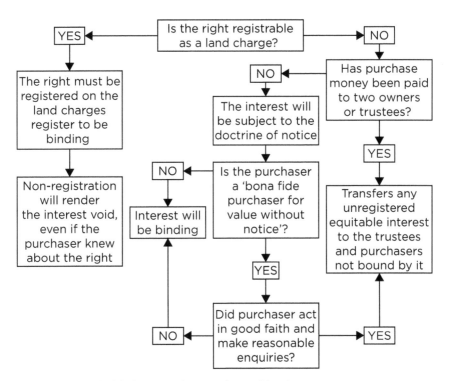

Figure 2.2: Equitable interests in unregistered land

As a final note, it is important to remember that once the unregistered land has been registered then these rules will cease to apply, except for any interests listed in the Land Registration Act 2002 as interests that override first registration, but we will consider those in greater detail in **Chapter 3**.

■ KEY POINT CHECKLIST

This chapter has covered the following key knowledge points. You can use these to structure your revision around, making sure to recall the key details for each point, as covered in this chapter.

• **Unregistered land** is land that has not been registered and there is no record of this on the central register held by HMLR.

• **The role and importance of title deeds**. You will need to be aware of what could happen if title deeds are lost or destroyed and the class of title that HM Land Registry will grant in the event of this happening. Someone applying for registration for the first time may not be granted the best class of title, being title absolute, if some deeds are missing or incomplete.

• **Land charges** is a separate land registration system to the permanent record of registered land in England and Wales. Land charges specifically relate to legal and equitable rights that a new purchase may be bound by. It is designed to be a crossover provision to record these important third-party rights until the land has been registered.

• **Legal rights** are binding 'on the world' and any new purchaser will automatically be bound by them – this is whether they have had notice of them or not.

• **Equitable rights** are split into rights that can be registered as a land charge and those which cannot but are governed by the doctrine of notice. Registrable rights are separated into six different categories, shown in **Table 2.2**.

• **The doctrine of notice**. If the purchaser is a 'bona fide purchaser of the legal estate for value without notice', meaning that if they are an honest purchaser of the legal estate by paying valuable consideration and they have had no notice of any equitable rights, then they will not be bound by them.

• **Notice** of the equitable right will depend on whether the purchase has received actual notice, constructive notice, or implied notice. Constructive notice requires the purchasers to make 'reasonable enquiries' and so can be a subjective element of the doctrine.

• **Overreaching** offers a defence mechanism to a purchaser and allows them to take free of any unknown equitable interests providing that purchase money is paid to at least two legal owners, or a legal owner and a second appointed trustee. This will then place the third-party interest with the individuals rather than in the property.

■ KEY TERMS AND CONCEPTS

• title deeds (**page 26**)
• root of title (**page 26**)
• puisne mortgage (**page 30**)
• overreaching (**page 35**)
• trust of land (**page 35**)

■ SQE1-STYLE QUESTIONS

QUESTION 1

A client is purchasing a property which is currently unregistered. It had been legally owned by two individuals who have both died and the property is being sold by their son who is acting as their executor under the Will. The solicitor has received the title deeds and carried out a search on the Land Charges Register, which reveals a restrictive covenant. The solicitor is satisfied with the enquiries and searches and completes the transaction. The client then receives a letter from the daughter of the previous owners, claiming that she has an equitable interest in the property as she loaned some money to her parents to extend the property some ten years ago. She claims that she is owed £10,000 from the property.

Which of the following best represents the client's legal position?

A. This should have been registered as a Class F land charge. The solicitor completed the necessary searches which showed no Class F entry and so the client will not be bound by this.

B. This is an equitable interest that is subject to overreaching. The property was legally owned by two people and so the interest has been overreached and the daughter's equitable interest now vests in the purchase money and not the property. The client will not be bound by this.

C. This is an equitable interest that is subject to overreaching. It has not been overreached as the purchase money has not been paid to two legal owners or to trustees. The client will be bound by this unless he is a bona fide purchaser of the legal estate for value without notice.

D. The property was legally owned by two people but as the money has been paid to a trustee the interest has been overreached and this equitable interest now vests in the purchase money and not the property. The client will not be bound by this.

E. This is an equitable interest that is subject to overreaching. It has not been overreached as the purchase money has not been paid to two legal owners or two trustees. The client will be bound by this unless he is a bona fide purchaser of the legal estate for value without notice and he can demonstrate that he has acted in good faith, and reasonable enquiries have been made.

QUESTION 2

A client claims that she has an interest in a property which was previously owned by her ex-partner. The client states that they both entered into an estate contract specifying that she would be offered first refusal to purchase the property. The client has become aware that her ex-partner has recently sold the property and she is distraught at the thought of not being given the opportunity to buy the property from him.

Which of the following best represents the legal position of this client?

A. An estate contract is a legal interest and as such 'binds the world'. The new purchaser would be bound by the contract and the client can enforce the same.

B. An estate contact is an equitable interest which must be registered as a land charge to be enforceable. However, if the purchaser knew about the contract then they would be bound by it and the client can enforce the same.

C. An estate contact is an equitable interest which must be registered as a land charge to be enforceable. This will apply even if the purchaser knew of the existence of the contract. The purchaser will not be bound by it and the client cannot enforce the same.

D. An estate contract is a legal interest and as such 'binds the world'. However, it must still be registered as a land charge to be enforceable. The client cannot enforce the same.

E. An estate contact is an equitable interest which must be registered as a land charge to be enforceable. However, if the purchaser is a bona fide purchaser of the legal estate for value without notice then they will not be bound by it and the client cannot enforce the same.

QUESTION 3

A Building Society was granted a second mortgage over a piece of unregistered land before compulsory registration was introduced in the area. The title deeds to the property were retained by the first mortgagee. The mortgage has not been repaid in full and the Building Society have become aware that the property was recently sold. They wish to enforce the remaining mortgage against the new owner and claim they have a legal interest in the property which the new purchase is bound by.

Which of the following best reflects the legal position of the Building Society?

A. As this mortgage is a puisne mortgage, it is a legal interest and, as legal interests bind the world, it will be binding on the new purchasers.

B. As this mortgage is a puisne mortgage, it needs to be registered as a land charge to protect the mortgagees' legal interest.

C. As this mortgage is a puisne mortgage, it needs to be registered as a land charge to protect the mortgagees' legal interest. If it is not registered then it will be subject to the doctrine of notice.

D. As this mortgage is a puisne mortgage, it needs to be registered as a land charge to protect the mortgagees' legal interest. If it is not registered then the interest is void, even if the purchase has notice of the same.

E. As this mortgage is a puisne mortgage, it needs to be registered as a land charge to protect the mortgagees' legal interest. If it is not registered then the purchaser will be protected by overreaching if the purchase money was paid to two trustees.

QUESTION 4

A client is purchasing an unregistered property. The title deeds include a conveyance dated 18 January 1956 and an assent dated 6 May 1982. The conveyance contains a description of the property but no plan. The wording of the conveyance states: 'the property shown edged red on the plan contained within the conveyance dated 28 February 1955 and made between ...'. The solicitor has not been sent any other title deeds.

Which of the following best reflects the legal position?

A. The current owner has provided title deeds dating back at least 15 years and showing an unbroken chain of ownership. There is a description of the property which is all that is needed and the seller has proven that he has a good root of title.

B. The current owner has provided title deeds dating back at least 15 years and showing an unbroken chain of ownership. There is a description of the property but there must also be a plan to prevent there being any doubt being cast on the legitimacy of the title. The seller has not proven that he has a good root of title.

C. The current owner has provided title deeds dating back at least 15 years and showing an unbroken chain of ownership. There are no other requirements necessary and the seller has proven he has a good root of title.

D. The current owner has provided title deeds dating back at least 15 years and showing an unbroken chain of ownership. There is a description of the property but there must also be a plan to prevent there being any doubt being cast on the legitimacy of the title. The seller has not proven that he has a good root of title and the solicitor will need to ask to see the earlier conveyance to fully satisfy these requirements.

E. The current owner has provided title deeds dating back at least 15 years and showing an unbroken chain of ownership. There are no other requirements necessary and the seller has proven he has a good root of title. The solicitor should insist upon paying the purchase money to two trustees to prevent any doubt being cast on the legitimacy of the title.

QUESTION 5

A client has recently purchased an unregistered property from a sole legal owner. The legal owner had, however, died and so the purchase money was paid to two trustees who had been appointed by the will to deal with the deceased owner's legal affairs. Shortly after moving into the property, the client is visited by a family member of the deceased legal owner claiming that they had been living in the property up until six months ago when they left to go travelling. The family member claims to have an interest in the land under a trust as they had always paid for the maintenance and upkeep of the land. The property was completely vacant and there were no personal possessions in the same at the time the client inspected the same. The client wants to know if she will be bound by this claim of an interest in the land.

Which of the following best represents the legal position of the client?

A. The client has paid the purchase money to two owners or two trustees and this automatically overreaches any unknown third-party interest in the land. The client is not bound by the same.

B. As the legal estate was owned by a sole owner, the third-party interest must be registered as a land charge to be valid. If it has not been registered then it will not be binding on the client.

C. As the legal estate was owned by a sole owner, the third-party interest must be registered as a land charge to be valid. If it has not been registered then it will only be binding if the client did not make reasonable enquiries.

D. The client has paid the purchase money to two owners or two trustees, which does not automatically overreach any unknown third-party interest in the land, but the client will not be bound by the same if they can demonstrate that they made reasonable enquiries.

E. This right is a legal right and so continues to bind all future owners regardless of whether it has been registered or whether the client was aware of the same. The client will be bound by the third-party interest.

◼ ANSWERS TO QUESTIONS

Answers to 'What do you know already?' questions at the start of the chapter

1) False, the time required for a root of title is 15 years. The legal owner would only ever need to produce documents dating back more than 15 years if the document they have dates back further than 15 years or if the root of title document refers to older deeds which also form part of the root of title.

2) The correct answer was B. The title deeds have been lost and so she is unable to produce sufficient documentary evidence to prove her ownership. She will be able to provide a statutory declaration of her time of ownership, but as she does not have the actual deed to prove this then HM Land Registry will not be able to grant an absolute title.

3) The correct answer was A. Puisne mortgages are specifically excluded by the legislation and so is one of the only legal rights that must be registered as a land charge to be binding on a future owner.

4) The correct answer was E. Any equitable right that has been registered as a land charge will automatically bind a future purchaser, whether they have checked the Land Charges Register or not.

5) The correct answer was B. A puisne mortgage is a legal interest but as it is excluded by legislation as a legal interest in unregistered land it must be registered as a land charge to be binding on a future owner. The fact that the sale proceeds were paid to a single vendor is acceptable here as the doctrine of overreaching will not apply to unregistered land charges.

Answers to end-of-chapter SQE1-style questions

Question 1:
The correct answer was E. This is because the interest is one which is not a registrable land charge and so the doctrine of overreaching would have offered the client a defence mechanism. However, the money was not paid to two legal owners or two trustees and as such we then must consider the doctrine of notice to understand whether the client would be bound by this third-party equitable interest. Option A is incorrect as this is not a right which is classed as a family home right, which generally focuses on rights between married parties. Option B is incorrect as it does not matter that the land was owned by two people; what matters is who the money is paid to. The legal owners have died and so money cannot be paid to them, only their trustees or legal representatives. Option C is incorrect as it does not explore the doctrine of notice in enough detail. Option D is incorrect as, again, it does not matter who the money is paid to, but how many people it is paid to. It has only been paid to one trustee and so overreaching does not occur.

Question 2:
The correct answer was C. This is because estate contracts are registrable equitable interests. Failure to register such an interest will deem it void, even if the purchase knows of its existence. Options A and D are incorrect as an estate contract is not a legal interest. Options B and C are incorrect as the law is very clear on the types of interests that must be registered to be enforceable, estate contracts are one of those interests and so it does not matter if the purchaser knew of this in any other way – if it is not registered then it is void.

Question 3:
The correct answer was D. This is because of similar reasons shown in question 2. This can however sometimes cause confusion when

there is mention of a mortgage as there can be an automatic assumption that they are always legal rights. The important point to note is that puisne mortgages will only arise in unregistered land and are a second or subsequent mortgage, which is why they are explicitly excluded by legislation as being a legal right.

Question 4:

The correct answer was D. A root of title is a deed which must show an unbroken chain of ownership dating back at least 15 years, but which also contains a recognisable description of the property and not cast any doubt on the legitimacy of the title. A missing plan would not meet these requirements as it does not provide an adequate description of the land in question. Option A is incorrect as a description of the land will include a plan. Option B is incorrect as it does not go far enough in the legal position of the question and further evidence is needed to fully satisfy the requirements of a good root of title. Option C is incorrect as it does not fully encompass the requirements of a good root of title and just going back 15 years is not enough. Option E is incorrect as this refers to overreaching an equitable right, which may be needed, but does not relate to the root of title to prove that this person owns the land they are selling.

Question 5:

The correct answer was A. This is because payment of the purchase money to two owners or two trustees is the safest way of preventing a new owner from being bound by unknown equitable interests. It is a defence mechanism for unknown equitable interests and so the doctrine of notice does not need to be considered if there is payment made in this way. This is why options B–E can be disregarded.

■ KEY CASES, RULES, STATUTES AND INSTRUMENTS

The SQE1 Assessment Specification does not require you to know any case names, or statutory materials, for the topic of land law. Despite this, you may find it useful to become familiar with these statutes:
Land Charges Act 1972
Law of Property Act 1925.

3

Registered land

■ MAKE SURE YOU KNOW

Compulsory registration of all land in England and Wales has been a fundamental change to land law and removes the issues faced by landowners if they lose their title deeds, but also clarifies some of the uncertainties around third-party interests.

You need to understand that the purpose of land registration is to capture not just the legal ownership but also the interests in that particular estate. HM Land Registry will keep a record of the land that has been registered and the purpose of keeping this centralised record goes much deeper than simply identifying who owns that piece of land.

As you will know from **Chapter 2**, the crossover from unregistered to registered land is still a work in progress and you will need to know which events will 'trigger' a first registration of that particular estate in land and then which future transactions will be registrable dispositions. These registrable dispositions work to try and keep an accurate record of the register of title so that any future purchaser is fully aware of what land they are buying and what interests or restrictions they will be bound by.

You will need to be aware of third-party interests such as notices or restrictions and the doctrine of overriding interests that we saw initially in **Chapter 2**. This doctrine still applies to registered land and although the category of overriding interests has been significantly reduced by the LRA 2002, it is important that you are aware of those overriding interests, in particular the doctrine of persons in actual occupation. There are of course exceptions to the rules of overriding interests including that a presumption of an overriding interest could be rebutted, or a purchaser can be protected by 'the overreaching the third-party right', all of which we will consider in detail in this chapter to enable you to tackle any question on the system of registered land.

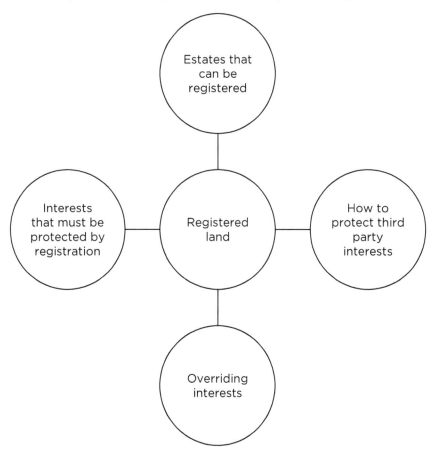

■ SQE ASSESSMENT ADVICE

As you work through this chapter, remember to pay particular attention in your revision to:
• estates that can be substantively registered
• how to protect third-party interests
• interests that need to be protected on the register
• interests that override registration.

■ WHAT DO YOU KNOW ALREADY?

Try answering these questions before reading this chapter. If you find some difficult or cannot remember the answers, make a note to look more closely at that subtopic during your revision.

1) What is the main purpose of land registration?
   a) to provide proof of legal ownership
   b) to make the register a complete and accurate record of the title
   c) to ensure the register is a complete and accurate reflection of the title of the land at any given time, so that it is possible to investigate title to land online
   d) to provide a future purchaser with confirmation of the boundaries of the property
   e) to provide details of any overriding interests in the land
   [Registered land, page 49]

2) True or false? Anyone who owns an estate in land, which remains unregistered, must apply to register the same with HM Land Registry before 2030.
   [Estates that can be substantively registered, page 50]

3) A client has contacted you to ask about compulsory registration of their land. They own a very large piece of land and are looking to sell a small piece of it to a neighbour who has been using it to park their car. She has been told by the neighbour that if she wants to sell this piece of land that she will have to register all of the land that she owns first. Is this true or false?
   [Registrable dispositions, page 51]

4) What is the purpose of a notice on the register of title?
   a) It details the burden of a third-party interest in the legal estate.
   b) It details specific terms that must be complied with on a registrable disposition of the legal estate.
   c) It details specific terms that must be complied with on a registrable disposition of the legal estate to ensure it is binding on any future owner.
   d) It details the burden of an overriding interest in the legal estate.
   e) It details the burden of a third-party interest in the legal estate to ensure it is binding on any future owner.
   [Interests that need to be protected by registration, page 54]

5) A lease granted for seven years or less will only be enforceable and binding against a new owner if it is registered against the register of title. True or false?
   [Overriding interests, page 56]

REGISTERED LAND

Whilst you will commonly hear of 'land' being registered, it is worth remembering that it is in fact the *estate* in land that is registered, so the freehold or leasehold estate. One parcel of land may have both a freehold and a leasehold estate registered against it, and so the purpose of this system of registration is to provide full details of each of these estates of land in England and Wales. The details are held on a central database and managed by the Land Registry.

This means that someone is able to request a copy of the register of title for that particular estate and see whether the land is freehold or leasehold, who owns the land and whether any rights, restrictions or third-party interests have been granted over that particular parcel of land. It means that all this information is in one place and eliminates the need for those paper title deeds considered in **Chapter 2**.

The register of title is the file which is held by HM Land Registry. There is one file held for every estate in land that is registered. The 'register' is split into three separate parts:

a) property register – confirms the legal estate, so whether it is freehold or leasehold, a description of the property and any rights it may benefit from, such as a right of way.

b) proprietorship register – confirms the name and address of the legal owners. It also details any restrictions which have been registered against the estate and burden the estate or legal owner.

c) charges register – contains notices of interests which burden the estate and need protection by registration, and details of any legal charges that have been granted over the land.

To ensure this accurate and up-to-date reflection of land ownership and rights is maintained, the Land Registration Act 2002 includes different categorisations of rights that can affect land. These are:

• substantively registrable estates
• registrable dispositions
• other third-party interests capable of protection on the register
• unregistered interests which override the registered estate.

The SQE requires you to know about the system of registered land and how different rights can be protected. The four categories above will therefore be considered in more detail throughout this chapter.

Estates that can be substantively registered

As we briefly considered in **Chapter 1**, there are only two types of legal estates available today. Those are freehold (forever) and leasehold (for a fixed term). Only legal estates are capable of being **substantively registered**.

Key term: substantively registered

This means that a piece of land will have a unique title number which is generated upon the first registration of that land.

Failure to substantively register a legal estate will mean the transfer is void and the seller of that land will hold the land for the purchaser on a **bare trust**.

Key term: bare trust

If substantive registration does not take place then the property will continue to remain in the legal ownership of the previous owner; however, the new owner is entitled to the benefit of the property at any time providing they are 18 or over. Whilst this may not seem too much of a problem, it can cause quite significant difficulties if the new owner wishes to resell the property, and so these trusts are best avoided by completing the substantive registration process.

The process of substantive registration shows the connection to unregistered land as an estate in land requires registration when a 'triggering event' occurs. The triggering events you need to know about are:

• any type of transfer of the land, whether this be a sale, a gift, inheritance or by court order
• the grant of a lease out of the freehold estate of more than seven years (or one which is to take effect more than three months after its grant)
• the creation of a protected first legal mortgage.

If any of these events occur with unregistered land then it will 'trigger' the first registration process. See **Figure 2.1**, in **Chapter 2**, for the different class of title that can be granted on first registration. **Practice example 3.1** shows the type of transaction that could be a triggering event.

Practice example 3.1

Elsie has owned her property since 1976 and has the original, and unregistered, paper title deeds to the land. There has never been a triggering event during her ownership. Elsie now wishes to give the property to her daughter, Delilah. Would this be a triggering event?

Yes, it would. This is a gift of the land from the original owner, Elsie, to a new owner, Delilah. It does not matter that it is between family members or that it is a gift of the land. The fact that the land is changing ownership means it must now be registered with HM Land Registry and this will then create the relevant freehold or leasehold legal estate in the land. The property will then also receive a unique reference number known as a title number.

Registrable dispositions

Once the relevant estate in land has been created (so freehold or leasehold) any future dealings with the land will be considered a **registrable disposition**. These are dealings with the land which will not be legally binding unless they are registered against the title of the property. They are:

- any transfer of a freehold or leasehold estate in land
- the grant of a lease out of any estate for a term exceeding seven years
- the grant or reservation of a legal easement
- the grant of a new or subsequent legal mortgage.

Failure to complete this registration process will mean the purchaser will acquire an equitable interest in the land only, which is very similar to the trust of land mentioned earlier in this chapter. The seller of the legal estate will retain the legal ownership but the purchaser will either have the right to acquire the formal legal title or legal right once substantive registration is completed, or have the right to benefit from the property, for example by receiving the sale proceeds if the property is sold.

Key term: registrable disposition

This relates to any transfer, sale, lease, legal easement or mortgage over land which already has a registered title. The relevant transaction must be registered to be protected, ie the disposition is *capable* of being registered.

Practice example 3.2 explains this in more detail.

Practice example 3.2

Marie has owned her property since 1976 and granted a legal mortgage on the estate in 2010. This was a triggering event and the estate was registered with HM Land Registry at that time. Marie has repaid the mortgage in full and now wishes to give the property to her daughter, Scarlett. Would this be a registrable disposition?

Yes, it would. It is a gift of the land from the original owner, Marie, to a new owner, Scarlett. It does not matter that it is between family members or that it is a gift of the land. The fact that the land is changing ownership means it is a registrable disposition and must be registered with HM Land Registry to protect Scarlett's legal ownership. If it is not registered then Scarlett would not be shown as the legal owner of the land and therefore would not be able, for example, to sell it in the future.

The importance of having these registrable dispositions correctly registered is so that any future purchaser of that land is clear on what the legal estate is (freehold or leasehold), that they know who owns the land and what, if any, other third-party interests affect the land. **Figure 3.1** shows these registration principles referred to above, but before you consider figure 3.1, you must be familiar with and understand two key terms: **third-party interests** and **overriding interests**.

Key term: third-party interests

A landowner may grant a right or a benefit over the land to someone who is not a legal or an equitable owner of the land. Examples are a right of way over the land to a neighbour or an agreement that the landowner will maintain boundaries for the benefit of a third party. These should be recorded on the register of title to be enforceable.

Key term: overriding interests

These are also rights or a benefit to someone who is not a legal or an equitable owner of the land and they will not appear on the register of title. Despite not appearing on the register of title these rights are still binding on both the current legal owner and any future purchaser. Examples are an equitable interest of a third party who has contributed to the purchase price of the land and therefore has the benefit of a constructive trust.

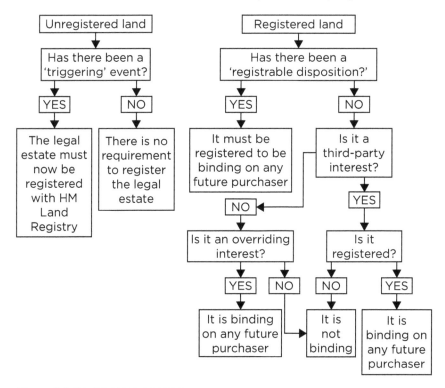

Figure 3.1: Registration principles

So, as you will see from **Figure 3.1**, there are some interests in land that must be registered to be binding on a future purchaser and some, such as overriding interests, which will be binding whether they are registered or not.

Exam warning

The SQE may ask you whether certain types of interests are binding on the new owner of a property if it is sold. Firstly, you will need to work out what type of interest it is; a third-party interest or an overriding interest. Then follow the rules laid out in the section below to see if the new owner is bound by the interest in question.

HOW TO PROTECT THIRD-PARTY INTERESTS

A third party can have some form of legal or equitable interest in a piece of registered land which is owned by someone else. Those interests are as follows:

• estate contracts
• freehold restrictive covenants

- equitable leases
- equitable easements and profits (created post 2003)
- equitable mortgages
- home rights
- trusts of land.

Interests that need to be protected by registration

All third-party rights are either capable of being protected by an entry in the register of title or they will be overriding. We will consider overriding interests later in the chapter.

Exam warning

If the right is capable of being protected by an entry on the register, but it has not been protected in this way, then it will not be binding against a future owner and loses its priority.

These interests must be registered by either:
- registration of a **notice** in the charges register
- registration of a **restriction** in the proprietorship register.

The right will not be binding on a future purchaser if it is not registered, *even if the purchaser knew of the interest*.

Key term: notice

A notice is an entry in the register which outlines the burden of a third-party interest in the legal estate.

Key term: restriction

A restriction is an entry in the register which specifies that a disposition of the land can only take place if certain terms of the restriction are complied with.

Table 3.1 sets out how the third-party interests mentioned above will need to be protected in the register of title.

Table 3.1: Third-party interests that need to be protected by the register of title

Estate contracts	Notice
• Freehold restrictive covenants	Notice
• Leasehold restrictive covenants	Restriction
• Equitable leases	Notice
• Equitable easements and profits (created post 2003)	Notice
• Home rights	Notice
• Equitable mortgages	Notice
• Trusts of land	Restriction

Revision tip

Do not confuse a notice on the charges register with the doctrine of notice discussed in **Chapter 2**. These are completely different principles. The first deals with a way in which to register and protect a third-party interest in registered land, the second, a complex principle setting out how to bind a third-party interest to a future purchaser unless they are a bona fide purchaser for value without notice.

Practice example 3.3 explains how these third-party interests can be binding on a future purchaser and how they should be registered to protect them.

Practice example 3.3

Florence has owned her property for five years. When she purchased the property, the following events occurred:
• She entered into a restrictive covenant specifying that she would not run a business from the premises.
• Florence's friend, Jess, moved in with her when she purchased the property and whilst Jess is not a legal owner (ie, she is not named on the register of title) she did contribute to the purchase price. Florence and Jess entered into a declaration of trust deed specifying the shares of their equitable (financial) ownership which also included a term that, if the property were to be sold, the solicitor handling the transaction needed to obtain authority from Jess before the sale proceeds were split.
• Florence also granted a mortgage to the Tyne and Wear Building Society, but that has not yet been registered as a legal charge. Florence is now selling the property.

How should these third-party interests be protected to ensure they are binding against a future purchaser?

- **If this is a freehold estate, the restrictive covenant must be registered as a notice in the charges register, this means that any purchaser is aware of it and must comply with it as the future owner of the estate.**
- **The trust deed between Florence and Jess must be registered as a restriction in the proprietorship register, this means that Florence will not be able to conduct any registrable disposition (so sell the property) unless the solicitor can confirm that the terms of the restriction have been complied with.**
- **The mortgage is a registrable disposition and so should be registered as a legal charge. If that has not happened then this would turn the legal mortgage to an equitable mortgage and Tyne and Wear Building Society must register this as a notice in the charges register for it to be binding on any future purchaser.**

Failure to register these interests as either a restriction or a notice will mean that a future purchaser will not be bound by the interest; this is regardless of whether they knew about them or not.

Now that we have seen how certain third-party interests need to be dealt with, we must consider the second type of potentially binding interest: overriding interests.

Overriding interests

In contrast to those interests that must be registered to be binding, an overriding interest will still bind a purchaser even if it does not appear on the register of title and whether they knew about them or not. Overriding interests fall into the following categories:
- easements and profits
- short-term legal leases
- interests of persons in actual occupation.

Easements and profits

You may think that these should not belong here, especially as a legal easement is a registrable disposition and so should be registered to be protected, which is correct where the easement has been granted expressly out of the registered legal estate. However, there are limited circumstances where easements and profits can be overriding interests; these are set out below:

- Any easement which was an overriding interest prior to LRA 2002 coming into force will continue to be an overriding interest, no matter how it was created.
- Any new legal easement impliedly created by s 62 LPA 1925.
- Any new legal easement created under the rule in *Wheeldon v Burrows*.
- Any new legal easement created by necessity, common intention or by prescription.

The final three points are considered in significant detail in **Chapter 6**, and it is recommended that you revisit this chapter once you have considered easements in full.

If dealing with a question of this type in the exam as part of registered land, you may be asked to determine whether the legal easement is overriding and as such, at this point, we will briefly consider the ways in which an easement would not convert to an overriding interest. Those are:

- It is not within the actual knowledge of the new purchaser.
- It would not have been obvious on a reasonably careful inspection of the land.
- The easement or profit has not been exercised within the past 12 months.

Practice example 3.4 explains how this scenario may arise.

Practice example 3.4

Clare owns a large plot of land and there is a small footpath to the far side of her land which allows access to a local nature reserve. It is only accessible by the neighbouring land but it is extremely overgrown and the neighbour, Nicola, has other means of accessing the nature reserve and has not used this footpath for many years. It would not be easy to see the footpath on inspection of Clare's land as there is a row of trees in front of the footpath. Clare sells her land to Beverly. Nicola wants to start using the footpath, but there is no mention of this right in the register of title. Would this right override Beverley's ownership meaning she is bound by it?

It is very unlikely Nicola would be successful in claiming this as an overriding interest. Whilst a right of way is capable of being a legal easement, it has not been created in any of the ways set out above and it does not meet the specific requirements to allow it to be

overriding, those being: the existence is not known by Beverly, the right was not obvious on a reasonable inspection of the land and Nicola had not used the right of way in the previous year.

Figure 3.2 considers the steps to be aware of if you are faced with a question of this type.

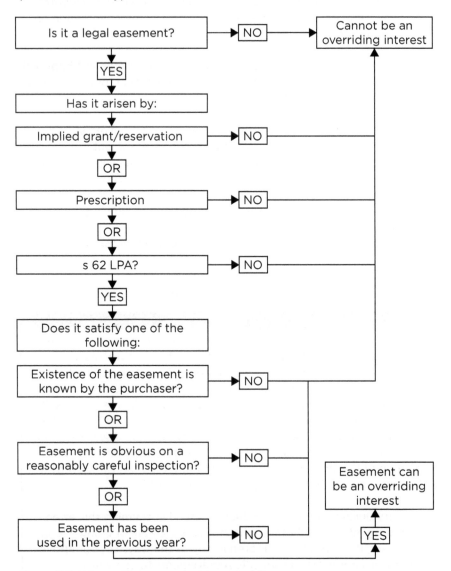

Figure 3.2: When will an easement be overriding

Outside of these limited circumstances, LRA 2002 expressly excludes equitable easements and profits and so they must be protected by notice on the register of title to be binding on a new purchaser.

Short-term leases

Leases granted for seven years or less are overriding interests and will automatically bind a future purchaser, whether they had knowledge of the lease or not. This only relates to legal leases and not equitable leases, which must still be registered to be binding. Equitable leases may, however, be overriding if the tenant is in actual occupation, which we will consider next.

Persons in actual occupation

This generally relates to every person who is in actual occupation (so living in the property) but who are not legal owners of the estate. A third party in actual occupation may be able to demonstrate an overriding interest in the estate. Whether a party is in 'actual occupation' is a question of fact and what is required is a physical presence on the land. Some periods of temporary absence are unlikely to affect 'actual occupation' but the intentions of the parties would then need to be considered to demonstrate this interest has arisen.

Figure 3.3 shows the steps to consider when dealing with any question of this type, which we will then consider in detail.

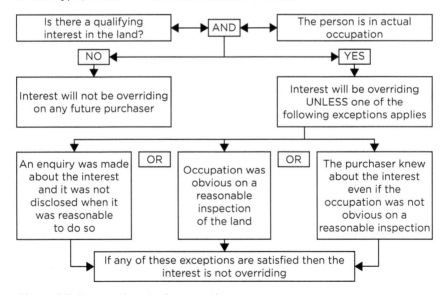

Figure 3.3: Persons in actual occupation

If any of the three exceptions are satisfied then the interest will not be binding on a purchaser of the estate. The example shown in **Practice example 3.5** explains this process in more detail.

Practice example 3.5

Florence and Jess have lived in the property for eight years. The estate is still registered in Florence's sole name and she granted a new mortgage to the North Tyne Bank two years ago which has been registered as a legal charge. Florence has defaulted on the mortgage and the bank wish to seek a possession order of the property. Jess has argued that she has a legal interest in the property due to her initial financial contribution to the purchase price. She is occupying the home and was also present in the property when the valuation was carried out. She argues that the bank are bound by her interest, which is overriding on their registered legal charge. Are the bank bound by the interest of Jess?

This is very typical of any case law dealing with this issue and the answer is yes. Jess holds a contribution based equitable interest under a trust of land (if registered as a restriction on the title deeds then this would be an express trust) and she is in actual occupation of the land, which would have been further strengthened if a valuation was carried out at the time Jess was present. If the bank have done nothing to enquire into that occupation then they would not be protected by any of the exceptions. If they seek a possession order and an order for sale is granted, they would have to ensure Jess is compensated financially for her contribution.

Revision tip

There are only a few interests in land which are expressly excluded by statute as being a proprietary interest and those are, interests under the Settled Land Act, legal leases taking effect three months from the date of grant and home rights under the Family Law Act. Other than these any proprietary interest in land can amount to a qualifying interest to satisfy the first limb of this test.

The meaning of 'actual occupation'

The meaning of 'actual occupation' is not defined in statute and so is something that has been considered in case law. **Table 3.2** sets out a number of these cases to illustrate how the meaning of 'actual occupation' can be determined if required in the SQE exam. You do not need to memorise the names.

Table 3.2: Key cases on actual occupation

Case name	Facts
Williams and Glyn's Bank v Boland [1981]	Legal title to the home was in the husband's sole name. Mrs Boland held an equitable interest in the home due to her financial contributions. The Court of Appeal held that Mrs Boland was in actual occupation and what was required was evidence of a 'physical presence' on the land.
Abbey National v Cann [1991]	Mr Cann purchased a property, claiming it would be for his sole occupation but his mother, Mrs Cann, and her partner would also be residing there. His mother contributed to the purchase price, obtaining a proprietary interest in the property. Mrs Cann was on holiday abroad when completion of the purchase took place and did not move into the property until she returned. Mr Cann defaulted on the mortgage repayments. The court held that Mrs Cann was not in 'actual occupation' at the date of completion and so her interest did not override that of the bank.
Chhokar v Chhokar [1984]	A property was purchased in Mr Chhokar's sole name but both parties contributed to the purchase price and upkeep of the property meaning that Mrs Chhokar obtained a proprietary interest in the property. Without her knowledge Mr Chhokar made arrangements to sell the property which took place whilst she was in hospital giving birth. She returned home to find she was locked out. The Court held she had an overriding interest and was in actual occupation despite her absence. Her possessions and furniture remained in the house and she had every intention to return home.
AIB v Turner [2016]	Mrs Turner resided in Barbados and had made the decision to live permanently outside of the UK, however she did return to the UK home occasionally. Her furniture remained in the property but her personal possessions had been removed. The Court held there was nothing 'actual' about her occupation and her interest was not overriding.

The 'actual occupation' of a person is clearly subjective in its nature, but the court will look for evidence that the occupation is continuous and permanent. Even if there are short periods of absence, this does not mean there is no actual occupation, provided there is a clear intention to return.

Exam warning

Remember, if dealing with a question of this type, there must be a proprietary interest AND actual occupation for the overriding interest to be successful initially. It is only then that you go on to consider the exceptions.

Protection from third-party interests

It may seem unfair for a new owner to be bound by third-party rights which they are unaware of and so there are certain ways they can be protected from this.

Overreaching

The SQE1 Assessment Specification does not expressly state that we need to consider overreaching as part of registered land; however, it has very strong connections to how a new purchaser can be protected from these unknown third-party interests and so we feel it is important to go over some of the information from **Chapter 2** here.

Overreaching is a defence mechanism, ensuring a new legal owner is not bound by an unknown third-party interest. Providing the sale proceeds or mortgage advance is paid to two legal owners, or two trustees of the estate; this will transfer any third-party interest in that estate over to the legal owner or to the trustees instead. This means that a purchaser or more commonly, a mortgagor, can take free of these unknown third-party interests and will not be bound by them. **Practice example 3.6** explains this in more detail.

Practice example 3.6

Mr and Mrs Flegg used £18,000 of their own money to purchase a property with their daughter and her husband, Mrs and Mr Maxwell-Brown, who granted a mortgage to the City of London Building Society. The property was meant for all of them to live in but the title deeds were registered in the names of Mrs and Mr Maxwell-Brown. Mrs and Mr Maxwell-Brown then defaulted on the mortgage.

The bank wish to repossess the property but can the Fleggs claim an overriding interest due to their proprietary interest and actual occupation?

These are the facts of *City of London Building Society v Flegg* [1988]. On the face of it, it would seem that yes, they satisfy all of the requirements of satisfying an overriding interest in the property. However, the mortgage money was paid to two legal owners, Mr and Mrs Maxwell-Brown, and as such this overreached the interest of Mr and Mrs Flegg and places their equitable interest with the Maxwell-Browns (who are now the trustees of that money) and not the property. The bank are not bound by this interest and to recover their money the Fleggs would have to sue the Maxwell-Browns for breach of trust.

Express agreement
As you can see, the development of case law has led to many changes, and processes have evolved which now require anyone in actual occupation of a property at the same time as the legal owner to sign a document confirming that they waive any rights in the property, which may be overriding, in favour of a mortgagee. This can of course sometimes be set aside if any undue influence is demonstrated.

■ KEY POINT CHECKLIST

This chapter has covered the following key knowledge points. You can use these to structure your revision around, making sure to recall the key details for each point, as covered in this chapter.

• You need to understand that the purpose of land registration is to capture not just the legal ownership but also the interests in that particular estate. Whilst HM Land Registry will keep a record of the outline of the land that has been registered, the purpose of keeping this centralised record goes much deeper than simply who owns that piece of land.
• The crossover from unregistered to registered land is still a work in progress. So, you will need to know which events will 'trigger' a first registration of that particular estate in land.
• Once an estate in land has been registered it is important to be aware of any future transactions that are registrable dispositions,

meaning an action by the landowner or by an interested third party that requires registration with HM Land Registry to ensure the disposition is accurately recorded on the register of title so that any future purchaser is fully aware of it.

• There are a number of third-party interests that can arise with an estate in land, such as estate contracts, restrictive covenants, mortgages and home rights to name a few. Some of these are minor interests and must be registered against the register of title to be enforceable by the person claiming that third-party interest. If they are not registered then they will not be enforceable, even if a future purchaser was aware of them.

• These third-party interests can be registered as notices or restrictions. The difference is an important one as restrictions will usually prevent a registrable disposition taking place unless certain terms are complied with. Most third-party interests will need to be registered as a notice to be enforceable.

• Whilst it may seem unequitable and goes against the purpose of having a central register with all rights and interests recorded in one place, the doctrine of overriding interests still applies to registered land. However, the category of overriding interests has been significantly reduced by the LRA 2002.

• Ensure you are aware of those overriding interests, in particular the doctrine of persons in actual occupation and remember the person claiming the overriding interest must have a qualifying interest in land and that they are in actual occupation of the property, which as you will see from the case law can be quite subjective.

• Finally, there are of course exceptions to the rules of overriding interests and these can be rebutted if any of the exceptions apply or a purchaser can be protected by overreaching the third-party right and paying money to two trustees.

■ KEY TERMS AND CONCEPTS

• substantively registered (**page 50**)
• bare trust (**page 50**)
• registrable dispositions (**page 51**)
• third-party interests (**page 52**)
• overriding interests (**page 52**)
• notice (**page 54**)
• restriction (**page 54**)

■ SQE1-STYLE QUESTIONS

QUESTION 1

A solicitor is acting for the buyer of a freehold property with registered title. The solicitor is aware that there is a non-owner occupier in the property and there is a trust deed in place specifying what should happen to the sale proceeds between the current legal owner and this third party.

What will the buyer's solicitor look for when examining the register of title to the property to confirm that this third-party interest is properly registered?

A. a notice referring to the trust deed in the Property Register

B. a notice referring to an easement in the Proprietorship Register

C. a restriction referring to the trust deed in the Charges Register

D. a restriction on dealings in the Proprietorship Register

E. a restriction on dealings in the Charges Register.

QUESTION 2

A solicitor has recently completed the purchase of a property for their client. The client has contacted the solicitor in a very distressed manner stating that his neighbour has started to use a path at the rear of his garden to access the local woods. When challenged, the neighbour informed him that he has an easement allowing him to do this which he granted to himself when he sold the land in 2000 and he has used the path every week since that time. There is nothing within the register of title which mentions this easement.

Which of the following best represents the client's legal position?

A. The easement must be registered as a notice within the Charges Register of the register of title to be enforceable.

B. Any easement which was an overriding interest prior to 2003 will continue to be an overriding interest and so will be binding on the client.

C. The easement must be registered as a restriction within the Proprietorship Register to be enforceable.

D. Any easement which was an overriding interest prior to 2002 will continue to be an overriding interest and so will be binding on the client.

E. The easement must be registered as a notice within the Property Register to be enforceable.

QUESTION 3

A woman has owned a property in her sole name for the past ten years. At the time of the purchase, she granted a mortgage over the property to a Building Society. Five years ago, her partner moved in with her and contributed significantly to some extensive renovations to the property. One year ago, the woman and her partner separated and six months ago the partner moved out, but left all his personal belongings, hoping that they would reconcile, and he would then return to the property. The woman lost her job three months ago and has not been able to repay the mortgage. The Building Society are considering their legal position and may seek possession of the property. The partner has contacted a solicitor for advice.

Which of the following best reflects the partner's legal position?

A. The partner can demonstrate that he has an equitable interest in the property by his financial contribution, but this will not override the interest of the Building Society as he is not currently in actual occupation of the property.

B. The partner does not have any equitable interest in the property. He would have to make a claim to the small claims court to recover any money he has invested into the property.

C. The partner can demonstrate that he has an equitable interest in the property by his financial contribution, but this will not override the interest of the Building Society as he was not in actual occupation of the property at the time of completion.

D. The partner can demonstrate that he has an equitable interest in the property by his financial contribution, and this will override the interest of the Building Society as he has left his belongings and has an intention to return to the property.

E. The partner does not have any equitable interest in the property, however if he moves back into the property before any legal action is taken by the Building Society he will be able to claim that he is in actual occupation and prevent any sale from taking place.

QUESTION 4

A client has contacted his solicitor following the purchase of his first property to say that a woman has recently attended the property and was very surprised to see that it had been sold. She expressed that she has an interest in the property as she contributed towards the mortgage and general upkeep of the property for five years whilst she lived there with the previous owner. She has been away to university for five months but always intended to return and states that this is her home. This woman was not named as a legal owner and there was no notice or restriction in the title deeds mentioning this supposed interest. The solicitor knows that a general enquiry was made to the seller asking if there were any other occupiers, to which he replied 'no'. The client cannot recall seeing any possessions in the home that may have belonged to the woman.

How should the solicitor advise this client?

A. The woman can demonstrate that she has an interest in the property by way of her contributions. Any interests of this nature are automatically overriding and binding on a future purchaser. The client will be bound by her interest.

B. The woman can demonstrate that she has an interest in the property by way of her contributions. Interests of this nature must be registered as a restriction in the Charges Register to be binding on a future purchaser. As there was no mention of this in the register of title the client will not be bound by her interest.

C. The woman can demonstrate that she has an interest in the property by way of her contributions. She can also demonstrate that she is in actual occupation as she only left temporarily and had full intention to return. The client will be bound by her interest.

D. The woman can demonstrate that she has an interest in the property by way of her contributions. Interests of this nature must be registered as a restriction in the Charges Register to be binding on a future purchaser. As there was no mention of this in the register of title the client will not be bound by her interest.

E. The woman can demonstrate that she has an interest in the property by way of her contributions. She can also demonstrate that she is in actual occupation as she only left temporarily and had full intention to return. An enquiry was made about any third-party interest and the seller failed to disclose this. The client will not be bound by her interest.

QUESTION 5

A solicitor is acting on behalf of a client in the purchase of a house which is registered with HM Land Registry. The register of title reveals that the legal owner holds the property on trust for his two children, who are aged 18 and 21.

Which of the following should the solicitor ensure the purchase money is paid to, to ensure the client takes the house free of the beneficial interest of the children?

A. To the legal owner and an appointed second trustee.

B. To the children who are the beneficiaries of the trust.

C. Purchase money can only be paid to the legal owner.

D. To both the legal owner and the children who are the beneficiaries of the trust.

E. To a separate trust company on behalf of the children.

■ ANSWERS TO QUESTIONS

Answers to 'What do you know already?' questions at the start of the chapter

1) The correct answer was C. Whilst A, B and D could all be correct, as land registration does provide this information, these are not the main purpose of land registration and specifically the introduction of the Land Registration Act 2002. This aims to provide a complete and accurate reflection of the title in a move towards e-conveyancing and allow the investigation of title to be carried out online. E is incorrect as overriding interests are not recorded on the register of title.

2) This was false. The Government aims to achieve as close to 100% comprehensive registration by 2030; this does not mean that landowners must register their land by this date. The rules on compulsory registration, unless changed in the future, still only apply when a triggering event occurs. If there is no triggering event then there is no requirement to register the estate in land.

3) This was false. Whilst the sale of the piece of land is a registrable disposition and would fall under the compulsory registration provisions, this would only relate to that specific piece of land which

has been sold. It is possible to grant a separate estate out of an unregistered estate. It may be preferrable for the neighbour and their solicitor to deal with a sale of part of a registered estate, but it does not make it compulsory to register land that is not part of the registrable disposition.

4) The correct answer was E. Whilst A is also correct, E sets out the full extent of a notice, which is to detail the burden of any third-party interest but also to ensure it is binding on any future purchaser. B and C are incorrect as this describes a restriction. D is incorrect as overriding interests are never recorded on the register of title.

5) This was false. Leases granted for seven years or less are overriding interests and will automatically bind a future purchaser, whether they had knowledge of the lease or not.

Answers to end-of-chapter SQE1-style questions

Question 1:
The correct answer was D. This is because any legal interest which restricts the way in which the property is dealt with on a registrable disposition, such as how the sale proceeds are distributed, must be protected by way of a restriction in the Proprietorship Register. The answers referring to the Charges Register are incorrect as the only matters that can be recorded in the Charges Register are mortgages or other financial burdens secured against the property and other rights or interests, such as leases, rights of way or restrictive covenants. Likewise, the references to the Property Register are incorrect as that will usually only include details of the property such as the address, owners and when it was first registered and rights the property benefits from, such as rights of way.

Question 2:
The correct answer was B. This is because all legal easements are registrable dispositions and so to be enforceable they must be completed by registration and noted on the Charges Register as a notice. However, you need to be aware of the dates in this question. You are told that the easement was granted in 2000 and the neighbour has used the same every week since then. This would make the easement an overriding interest and it continues to be an overriding interest. This makes options A, C and E incorrect as they all refer to entries in the register of title, which is not required for an overriding interest. This provision applies to any overriding interest created before the Land Registration Act

(LRA) 2002 came into force. This is why option D is also incorrect as that states 2002, whereas the LRA 2002 did not actually come into force until 2003.

Question 3:

The correct answer was C. Again, this is a question where you need to pay close attention to the dates. To be an overriding interest in this way there has to be evidence of a qualifying interest in the land, which the partner could demonstrate by his financial contribution which will likely be a constructive trust. However, this must also be coupled with actual occupation of the land, which must be at the time of 'completion'. Completion in this scenario will be the date the mortgage completed, which we know is before the partner moved in; as such, there is no way the Building Society could be aware of his occupation or make any relevant enquiries before the mortgage completed. Had the mortgage been granted after his occupation then this may very well be an overriding interest, especially if he could demonstrate his intention to return. This is why the other options are incorrect.

Question 4:

The correct answer was E. This is because the woman can demonstrate a third-party interest due to her contributions to the mortgage and general upkeep. She can also demonstrate that she was in actual occupation of the property due to her intention to return. However, one of the exceptions to the overriding rules applies here as a specific enquiry was made to the previous owner asking if there were any other occupiers. Leaving temporarily to go to university does not remove her occupation status and the fact that the previous owner failed to provide this information, when it was reasonable to expect him to do so, does mean that the client will not be bound by this third-party interest.

Question 5:

The correct answer was A. This is because, as the property is subject to a trust, the solicitor should ensure that they use overreaching to remove the beneficial interest held in the property and place it with the legal owner and a second appointed trustee. HM Land Registry permits a legal owner to appoint a second trustee simply for the purpose of overreaching. B, D and E are incorrect as we have no information about the trust – there could be conditions stating that the trust money is not paid to them until they reach a certain age. C is incorrect as the legal owner may be deceased or may have lost capacity; in that case the money would be paid to a suitable appointed person.

■ KEY CASES, RULES, STATUTES AND INSTRUMENTS

The SQE1 Assessment Specification does not require you to know any case names, or statutory materials, for the topic of land law. Despite this, you may find it useful to become familiar with these statutes:

Land Registration Act 2002

Law of Property Act 1925.

4

Freehold estates

■ MAKE SURE YOU KNOW

This chapter will take you through the essential characteristics relating to freehold estates in land and the other ways in which they can be transferred. **Chapter 5** will then focus on leasehold estates.

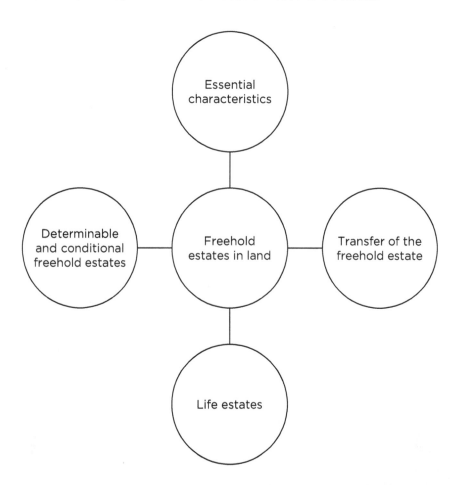

We need to consider these estates in land in this way as we already know there are two legal estates in land: freehold and leasehold. It is important to remember that it is perfectly possible for there to be both a freehold and a leasehold estate in a single piece of land. This would occur where person A owns the freehold estate of a piece of land and grants a 50-year leasehold estate in that same piece of land to a tenant, person B. The tenant would have all their legal rights and rights of occupation under the lease but that piece of land has those two separate estates: the freehold owned by person A and the leasehold owned by person B. At the end of that 50-year term, if the lease is not renewed then the leasehold estate would expire and the freehold estate would be the only one remaining.

This further demonstrates the purpose of land registration and that the title register is not just intended to reflect who the legal estate owner is of a specific piece of land, but more importantly, what rights and interests exist in that piece of land.

■ SQE ASSESSMENT ADVICE

As you work through this chapter, remember to pay particular attention in your revision to:
• the basic principles of freehold estates in land
• life estates
• determinable and conditional freehold estates
• how to transfer the freehold estate.

■ WHAT DO YOU KNOW ALREADY?

Try answering these questions before reading this chapter. If you find some difficult or cannot remember the answers, make a note to look more closely at that subtopic during your revision.
1) A freehold estate is a 'fee simple absolute in possession'; what is meant by 'fee simple'?
   a) The estate will last forever.
   b) The estate will last for a fixed number of years.
   c) The estate will automatically come to an end on the death of the legal owner.
   d) The estate will pass to any beneficiaries of the estate owner upon their death.

e) The estate will automatically revert to the Crown on the death of the legal owner.

[The freehold estate, page 75]

2) The owner of a freehold estate in land is currently travelling the world and has granted a short lease to a third party who is paying rent monthly. The owner cannot satisfy that they have a fee simple absolute in possession as they are not currently residing in the property. True or false?

[The freehold estate, page 75]

3) A client wishes to purchase a piece of land which contains a restrictive covenant specifying that there can be no building work carried out on the land. The client is concerned about this and feels there has been misrepresentation on behalf of the seller who told him the land was freehold and so should be free of any encumbrances. What would be the most appropriate advice to give to this client?

a) An owner of freehold land has absolute ownership and so there can be no third-party restrictions.

b) An owner of freehold land has absolute ownership but there may still be restrictions on the land; however, this restriction is too draconian and can be ignored.

c) An owner of freehold land with a fee simple absolute in possession has the closest possible form of absolute ownership; however, this does not mean it is completely free from encumbrances and there may be restrictive covenants which still apply to the land.

d) An owner of freehold land does not have to comply with any third-party restrictions.

e) An owner of freehold land must only comply with any third-party restrictions if they are residing on the land and are 'in possession' of the same.

[The freehold estate, page 75]

4) A client, Marie, has contacted you as she and her brother were granted a life interest in a property for their joint lives. Her brother has just been told he has an incurable illness and a very short life expectancy and so Marie wishes to sell the property now before he dies. Marie has found a purchaser to buy the property and believes the life interest will remain in place until her death. True or false?

[Life estates, page 77]

5) A determinable fee simple will only terminate the ownership of the freehold legal estate if a specific but unpredictable event occurs. True or false?

   [Determinable and conditional fee simple, page 79]

THE FREEHOLD ESTATE

All land in England and Wales is owned by the Crown, from which different estates of separate parcels of that land have been granted to individuals. There are now only two legal estates in land, those being freehold and leasehold.

The most common description for a freehold estate is fee simple absolute in possession. This is the closest possible way that an individual can own a parcel of land with the guarantee that it will never pass back to the ownership of the Crown unless the legal owner should die intestate with no family to inherit the freehold estate. The only situation that you will find a freehold estate in land being passed back to the ownership of the Crown is when there is no family to inherit the estate.

It's important we understand what this means, so it is worth looking at how the term 'fee simple absolute in possession' breaks down:

a. Fee simple: The owner of that parcel of land has the right to use and enjoy the land for their lifetime and they are free to transfer, sell or otherwise have any dealings with the land, such as granting a mortgage, a leasehold estate, or rights to third parties. They can also transfer the land under their Will.

b. Absolute: The ownership of the land is not conditional, for example it will transfer to them if they marry, nor can the ownership end on the occurrence of some specific event such as getting divorced. The right of ownership is absolute.

c. In possession: The owner is entitled to take immediate possession and can occupy and enjoy the land. In possession also means the right to receive rent from the land and so even if a tenant is in possession, the owner will be entitled to the rent and does not lose 'possession' in that way.

This may seem a very long-winded way of explaining freehold ownership, but this was important at the time it was introduced to show a clear distinction to other forms of ownership that had been in existence prior to 1925. **Figure 4.1** shows how this ownership of a freehold estate in land operates.

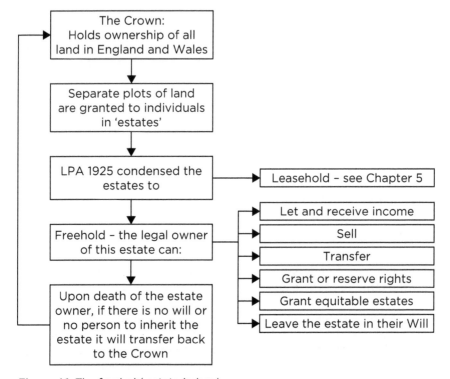

Figure 4.1: The freehold estate in land

LIFE ESTATES

A life estate is the right to use or occupy a property during somebody's lifetime. An example of this would be if a parent decides to transfer their home to a child for the duration of that child's lifetime, following which the property may then be sold or transferred to someone else or it may transfer back to the parent.

Life estates can be separated into:
- fee simple absolute in remainder (ie, a future interest in the land) which would be the right of somebody to own or possess the land once the fixed term interest of the current owner expires, or
- fee simple absolute in reversion which would be the right of the original estate owner to own or possess the land again once the fixed term interest they have granted to a third party has expired.

Whilst life estates cannot exist as a legal estate, they are very common equitable interests (as discussed in **Chapter 1**) and they can only exist as an equitable interest behind a trust. These types of property rights that are granted 'for life' can be commonplace and will be determined by the life of a specific person, which means the life estate will come to an end at some unknown point in the future.

The person who has the benefit of the life interest is known as the **life tenant** and they will have the right to occupy the property and to generate income from the estate by renting it to a third-party tenant. They could also sell or transfer the land (with permission from the person who granted the life interest), but the terms of the life estate would still apply, meaning the ownership by that third party would end on the death of the life tenant or the death of another named third party, making this a rather undesirable investment for most people.

Key term: life tenant

The right by one or more persons to use or occupy property for their life. It is often granted to someone by a Will or trust deed.

The life tenant cannot leave the property in their Will for the obvious reason that their ownership will come to an end upon their death or the death of a third party, so there will be no estate to pass to a beneficiary. However, the rules of intestacy do apply and so if the original estate owner has died before the life tenant, then the property can be inherited like any other property. **Figure 4.2** explains a life estate in more detail.

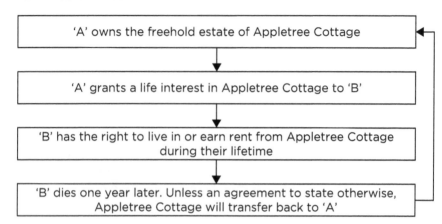

Figure 4.2: Life estates

Fee simple absolute in remainder

This is one way in which a freehold or leasehold estate owner can grant a life estate and upon the death of the life tenant the property will pass to another person specified by the original estate holder. This is a common provision for someone to include in their Will. **Practice example 4.1** shows this in practice.

Practice example 4.1

Dawn owns the freehold estate of a property and lives with her new partner, Riley. Riley does not own the property with Dawn but she would like him to remain living in the property after her death and then she would like the full freehold estate to pass to her two children from a previous marriage. How can Dawn be certain that her estate will be handled in this way?

This is a very common example of an estate in reversion. Once Dawn has died her partner Riley can continue to live in the property for the rest of his life. This is a trust which is an equitable interest in the property. Once Riley dies the full legal ownership of the property, so the fee simple absolute in possession, will transfer to Dawn's children.

Exam warning

If you are asked to determine whether a client has a legal freehold, you will need to show that all elements of 'fee simple absolute in possession' have been met. Meaning, they must be the owner of that piece of land, there must not be any conditions on their ownership, such as it coming to an end on the occurrence of some specific event and they must be in possession, which includes receiving rent from the land. If the scenario given does not fit these exact specifications then it is likely the ownership will be an equitable interest only.

Fee simple absolute in reversion

Again, a very similar concept to a fee simple in remainder, however the legal estate is never transferred to anyone else and remains with the estate owner. Very simply, the estate owner grants a life interest to a third party. Once that person has died, the full 'fee simple absolute in possession' transfers back to the estate owner. Whilst the legal estate is held by the life tenant, the estate owner holds a 'fee simple absolute in reversion' of the property, rather than the fee simple absolute in possession.

One important difference is that an estate in reversion can arise by implication and when a life estate is created in this way, but there is no express agreement as to what should happen with the same once the life tenant has died, then it will automatically transfer back to the original estate owner.

Determinable and conditional fee simple

Owners of an absolute freehold estate are free to transfer all or part of that freehold estate at any time during their ownership. There can be situations where that absolute ownership can be cut short by a specified event or if certain conditions not being met.

Whilst these types of freehold estates should have been abolished by the Law of Property Act 1925, there is still a possibility that you will come across this type of ownership and so it is important to still mention them here.

Determinable fee simple

Quite simply, this will automatically terminate the ownership of the freehold legal estate if a specific but unpredictable event occurs, which would have to be specified at the time of the original transfer of the freehold estate to the estate owner. **Practice example 4.2** explains this in more detail.

Practice example 4.2

Jennifer has agreed to transfer the absolute freehold title in her property to her son, David. This is on the following terms: 'the property will be transferred in fee simple until David wins the national lottery'. What will happen if David does win the lottery?

The ownership by David will be cut short if he wins the national lottery in his lifetime. The ownership of the freehold title would then automatically transfer back to Jennifer.

Revision tip

Try not to confuse a determinable fee simple with a life interest. On the face of it they seem very similar; however, the major difference is that a determinable fee simple will take effect on a specific but *unpredictable* event. Death is unfortunately a very certain event which will happen to everyone. Winning the lottery is not a certain event. If a determinable fee simple is granted to take effect upon the death of the estate owner then that would have the effect of creating a life interest.

Conditional fee simple

Very similar in nature to a determinable fee simple but requires a condition to be complied with throughout the ownership of the person to whom the estate is transferred. Again, **Practice example 4.3** explains how this could work in practice.

Practice example 4.3

Jennifer has agreed to transfer the absolute freehold title in her property to her son, David. This is on the following terms: 'the property will be transferred in fee simple on the condition that David never gets divorced'. What would happen if David does get divorced?

Should David breach this condition during his ownership then he loses the right to continue with his ownership of the land.

The main difference between a determinable and a conditional fee simple is the different rights of the person who has granted the estate. In the above examples, if the determinable event takes place then the estate will come to an end automatically. However, if David breaches the condition of divorcing then it will be up to Jennifer to decide if she wishes to bring the estate to an end and it will not happen automatically.

How to transfer a freehold estate in land

Regardless of the way in which this legal estate is acquired or transferred it must be created by a deed. S 1(2) of the Law of Property (Miscellaneous Provisions) Act 1989 (L(MP)A) sets out the formal requirements of a deed, which are:

• It is clear on the face of it that it is intended to be a deed
• It is validly executed as a deed by the parties that are subject to it.

For a legal estate, this deed must also be registered for the legal estate to be formally transferred from a seller to a purchaser, which we considered in detail in **Chapter 3**. The mechanics of how land is transferred at HM Land Registry is outside the scope of this book and is part of the conveyancing process.

Exam warning

Even if you have been able to satisfy all elements of 'fee absolute in possession' on behalf of a client and you can demonstrate that there is a legal freehold estate, if the correct formalities of registration have not been complied with then that client may not hold the legal estate and may have an equitable interest only.

Regardless of the type of freehold ownership or how it has been transferred, the one common feature is there is no fixed end point of the ownership as no one knows when someone will sell the land or when the title holder(s) will die. This is the fundamental distinguishing feature from leasehold estates, which we will consider in detail in the next chapter.

Grant of a lease

Before you move onto leases, it is important to remember what we explained at the start of this chapter, which is that the owner of an absolute freehold estate (the fee simple absolute in possession) is permitted to do whatever they wish with that estate, this includes granting a lease to a third party.

As you will see from **Chapter 5**, a lease must always be granted for a specified length of time, and so once that time has expired, the leasehold estate will automatically be extinguished. During the term of the lease the owner has exclusive possession and they can dispose, transfer, or otherwise have any dealings with the leasehold interest for their ownership. However, that is just the leasehold interest and the freehold estate will continue to be in existence regardless of how many times the leasehold estate is sold or transferred. **Figure 4.3** shows how the owner of a freehold estate can grant a typical legal lease.

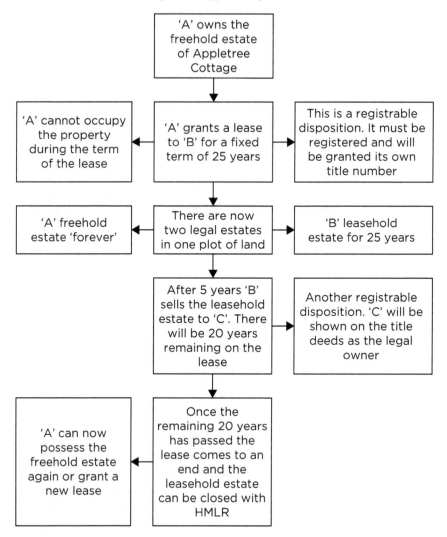

Figure 4.3: The grant of a lease

This is a basic overview of how the leasehold estate can be granted from the freehold estate and we will consider this in greater detail in **Chapter 5**. You may find **Figure 4.4** helpful as a final summary to understand the different types of estates and interests that can be granted from the freehold estate which will help you to answer this type of question in the SQE exam.

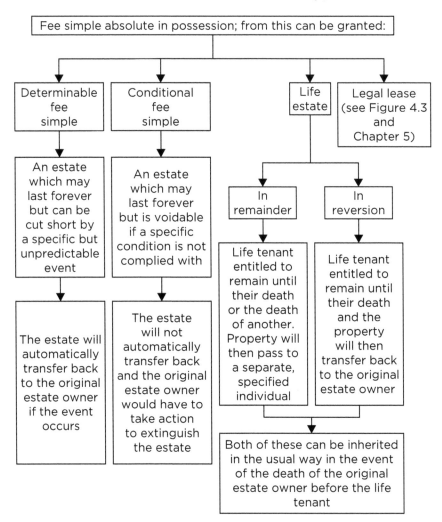

Figure 4.4: Types of estates and interests that can be granted from the freehold estate

■ KEY POINT CHECKLIST

This chapter has covered the following key knowledge points. You can use these to structure your revision around, making sure to recall the key details for each point, as covered in this chapter.

- The basic principles of the freehold estate. You must remember that to demonstrate the closest possible form of absolute ownership an individual will need to show that they have 'fee simple absolute in possession' of the piece of land in question.

- If an individual does satisfy all these requirements it does not mean that the land will be completely free from encumbrances. The same rules of rights, encumbrances and interests in land will still apply.
- Life estates are very common forms of freehold ownership. These are equitable interests, usually made under a trust deed or by a Will. The wording of these life interests is important to determine exactly when it will end.
- Look out for words which will indicate whether the grantee of the life estate has a fee simple absolute in reversion or in remainder. A reversion will always usually revert to the grantor upon the death of the life tenant. A remainder is likely to revert to a third party on the death of the life tenant.
- Also look out for words which may indicate that the freehold legal estate could be terminated or voidable on the occurrence or breach of some condition. Remember that a determinable fee simple will automatically terminate on the occurrence of a specific but unpredictable event whereas a conditional fee simple is voidable if a certain condition is breached, but it would be for the grantor to bring the legal estate to an end.
- The death of a person can never be a determinable factor and even though you may not know when death will occur, it is certain to happen at some point and so is not an unpredictable event.
- Regardless of the type of freehold estate that is held by a party, it must be created by a deed. For a valid legal estate, it must also be registered.
- A lease can be granted out of a freehold estate in land. This does not change that parcel of land to leasehold, but it does create a separate leasehold estate meaning that one parcel of land can be both freehold and leasehold at the same time.

■ KEY TERMS AND CONCEPTS

- life tenant (**page 77**)

■ SQE1-STYLE QUESTIONS

QUESTION 1

A client has been gifted a freehold estate in land from his uncle who has recently died. There were some specific terms of the gift including: 'the property will be transferred to my nephew until he marries'. The client is confused by what this means.

How should the solicitor advise the client when considering this term?

A. The client has been gifted the property and so will receive the fee simple absolute in possession; the term has no bearing on this type of ownership.

B. The client has been gifted the property but his ownership would be voidable when he marries.

C. The client has been gifted the property based on a life interest and he can remain in the property for the remainder of his life.

D. The client has been gifted the property but his ownership would be terminated automatically when he marries.

E. The client has been gifted the property but he is free to sell it and can do so providing he is not married when the sale takes place.

QUESTION 2

A client has sought legal advice following the death of her elderly neighbour. She has known the neighbour all her life and knew that he did not have any relatives. On his deathbed, he told her that he did not have a Will but wanted her to live in his property for the rest of her life as she was his only 'family'. The client would like to know how the property can be transferred to her.

Which of the following best represents the legal position?

A. The legal estate can be transferred providing that all formal requirements of a deed are met and the legal estate is registered.

B. The legal estate does not need to be transferred and the client can live there under the terms of the verbal agreement which would be a life estate. She can live there for the rest of her life and upon her death it will transfer to the neighbour's family under the intestacy rules.

C. The legal estate can be transferred but the client would hold a determinable fee simple estate and it would be terminated automatically upon the client's death.

D. The legal estate cannot be transferred unless all formal requirements of a deed are met. If so, then the interest created would be a life estate and upon her death it will transfer to the neighbour's family under the intestacy rules.

E. The legal estate cannot be transferred unless all formal requirements of a deed are met. If so, then the interest created would be a life estate and the client can live there for the rest of her life. and upon her death it will transfer to the Crown.

QUESTION 3

A client has recently purchased a freehold estate. He knew there had been a lease granted out of the freehold estate for a term of 55 years. The lease is due to expire next year but he wants to retain possession of the land now as he would like to redevelop the same. He wants to know how to remove the lease from the freehold estate.

How should the solicitor advise the client?

A. The client owns the fee simple absolute in possession of the freehold land and so is entitled to do whatever he likes with that land.

B. The client owns the fee simple absolute of the freehold land, but while there is a valid lease granted out of that freehold estate, he cannot take possession of the land. He would need to obtain a court order to remove the lease.

C. The client owns the fee simple absolute of the freehold land, but while there is a valid lease granted out of that freehold estate, he cannot take possession of the land. He would need to wait until the full term of the lease has expired before he can apply to close the leasehold title and obtain possession of the land.

D. The client owns the fee simple absolute of the freehold land, but while there is a valid lease granted out of that freehold estate, he cannot take possession of the land. He would need to obtain a court order to remove the lease.

E. The client owns the fee simple absolute in possession of the freehold land but would still need a court order to remove the lease.

QUESTION 4

Two clients have been granted a life estate in a freehold estate of land. The terms state: 'the property is transferred to the clients for their joint lives and will then pass to my uncle'.

Which of the following best represents the interest the clients hold in this freehold estate?

A. A determinable fee simple which is voidable upon the death of one of the clients.

B. A conditional fee simple which is voidable upon the death of both clients.

C. A fee simple in remainder which will transfer to the uncle upon the death of both clients.

D. A fee simple in remainder which will transfer to the uncle upon the death of one of the clients.

E. A fee simple in reversion which will transfer to the uncle upon the death of one of the clients.

QUESTION 5

A client owns a freehold estate in land and would like to allow his friend to live there for the remainder of the client's life. Once the client dies, he would like to transfer the freehold estate to his partner and allow her to live there for the remainder of her life before eventually transferring to his children.

Which of the following best represents the estate in land that the client should create?

A. A leasehold estate.

B. A fee simple in remainder.

C. A determinable fee simple.

D. A fee simple in reversion.

E. A conditional fee simple.

■ ANSWERS TO QUESTIONS

Answers to 'What do you know already?' questions at the start of the chapter

1) The correct answer was D. The owner of that piece of land has the right to use and enjoy it for their entire lifetime. Upon their death it can be transferred to anyone who is a beneficiary under a Will, or if there is no Will but the legal owner has qualifying family members, then it will transfer to them under the intestacy rules. There is no provision for an absolute freehold title to come to an end early or revert to the Crown unless the estate owner dies intestate and has no family who can inherit the estate.

2) The correct answer was false. The term 'in possession' does not strictly mean that the estate owner must always reside on the land. It

also means that they are permitted to enjoy the land, which includes receiving rent from the same. They do not lose 'possession' by renting the land to a third party.

3) The correct answer was C. Remember that the title register is designed to be a record of all legal rights and interests plus any equitable rights and interests. It is not simply a record of ownership. A and D are incorrect as whilst freehold land is the closest possible form of absolute ownership of land, there may still be numerous rights, restrictions and other encumbrances on the title deeds which must continue to be complied with. B is incorrect as it does not matter how draconian the restriction, if it is on the title deeds then it must be complied with unless it is discharged. E is incorrect as if the client is the legal owner then it does not matter that he is not 'in possession', he must still comply with the same.

4) The correct answer was false. The wording of the life estate is important here. It states the 'joint lives' of Marie and her brother and so it is only valid for as long as they are both living. Had the wording said 'for their lives' then it would last as long as either of them are alive. Notwithstanding that Marie will need permission to sell the house from the person who granted the life estate, she is also incorrect in her assumptions on how long this could last.

5) The correct answer was true. This is also the significant difference between a determinable fee simple estate and a life estate. To end a determinable fee simple, the event must be unpredictable, so there can be no guarantee that it will happen.

Answers to end-of-chapter SQE1-style questions

Question 1:

The correct answer was D. This is because this is an example of a determinable fee simple estate which terminates automatically on the occurrence of a specified event. As the uncle has already died, the property would then revert to the trustees. Option A is incorrect as the transfer would be subject to a trust which would include these terms and so it would always have a bearing on the ownership. Option B is incorrect as it refers to the ownership being voidable, which only applies to conditional fee simple estates. Option C is incorrect as this is not a life interest. Option E is incorrect as the client may well be able to sell the property but he would need the trustees' consent and the same terms would then apply to any other property he purchased with the sale money.

Question 2:

The correct answer was E. This is because whilst the intentions of the neighbour may have been to allow his friend to live in his property for the rest of her life, there can be no estate or interest created in land unless there is a deed which satisfies the formal requirements of a deed. If there is a deed then the client can live there for the rest of her life. Upon her death it will revert to the Crown as you are told that the neighbour has no family and no Will. Option A is incorrect as it does not go far enough to explain the full situation that the client faces. Option B is incorrect as there cannot be the creation of this type of interest in land verbally, and it must be by way of a deed. Option C is incorrect as the death of one party can never be a determinable condition. The event must be one that is specific but may never occur. Option D is incorrect as you have been told that there is no family to inherit the estate.

Question 3:

The correct answer was C. This is because a legal lease will have its own separate title number and is a separate legal estate. The owner of the freehold estate will be unable to take possession of the land during the term of the lease unless there is a breach of the terms of the lease, which we will consider in more detail in Chapter 5. Option A is incorrect due to the reasons already mentioned and options B, D and E are all incorrect as they refer to court orders, which would not be available to the client simply because he wants possession of the land.

Question 4:

The correct answer was D. This is because the use of the words 'their joint lives', means the estate will transfer to the uncle when one of the clients dies as they both need to be alive for the life interest to remain. Had he used the words 'for their lives', that would mean both of their lives as individuals. This is also an example of a fee simple in remainder as the estate will transfer to a specified third party once the life interest has come to an end. A is incorrect as a determinable fee simple can only be used for a specific but unpredictable event occurs, and although we don't know when death will occur, we know that it will definitely happen at some point. B and C are incorrect as the wording of the question makes it clear that it is on the death of one of the clients, not both. E is incorrect as the property will transfer to the uncle after the death of the clients, if it were to pass back to the original owner it would be a reversion, but as it goes to another third party it is in remainder.

Question 5:
The correct answer was B. This is because the life tenant is entitled to remain in the property until their or another's death, in this scenario that would be the client. The property will then transfer to a separate individual rather than reverting to the client (which would be an estate 'in reversion'). This can also be inherited by the client's children in the usual way if the client dies before the life tenant. The life interest would remain in place until the death of the partner, but the children would become the trustees of the same. A is incorrect as the only way to create a leasehold estate is by granting a lease of a fixed term. C and E are incorrect as there is no specified condition or determinable event which would change the ownership. D is incorrect as the property will pass to another third party after the death of the partner. If it was to transfer back to the original owner it would be a reversion, but as it passes to another person it is in remainder.

■ KEY CASES, RULES, STATUTES AND INSTRUMENTS

The SQE1 Assessment Specification does not require you to know any case names, or statutory materials, for the topic of land law. Despite this, you may find it useful to become familiar with these statutes:
Law of Property Act 1925
Law of Property (Miscellaneous Provisions) Act 1989.

5

Leasehold estates

■ MAKE SURE YOU KNOW

You will have seen from **Chapter 4** that a leasehold estate is always created out of a freehold estate, and this shows one of the key differences between the two legal estates: freehold estates are indefinite in their duration and a leasehold estate lasts for a fixed length of time; it can be ended once the fixed term has expired or any time before in certain circumstances.

A lease is something that most will have heard of and be familiar with, but leases can be used for different purposes. A shop owner may have a commercial lease for renting of business premises, a student may have a lease under a tenancy agreement in student accommodation or an individual can be the legal owner of a flat or house which is leasehold. The business owner and the student have no legal estate in that piece of land; they are, however, permitted to use it for a fixed time. The homeowner/flat owner does, however, have a legal estate in that specific parcel of land and they can dispose of or carry out any other registrable disposition with that leasehold estate during the term of the lease.

This chapter will focus on how we determine whether an individual has the right to use a specific parcel of land as a legal estate or whether they are permitted to use the land only for a short period of time. We will also look at lease clauses, covenants and the overall relationship between the landlord and tenant of a lease. Leases are a combination of a rich, but at times, complex set of arrangements and principles which you need to be aware of when tackling a question on a leasehold estate.

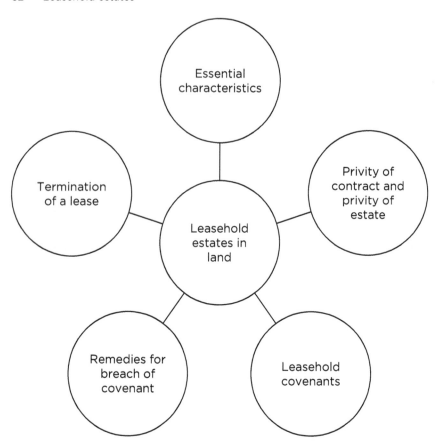

■ SQE ASSESSMENT ADVICE

As you work through this chapter, remember to pay particular attention in your revision to:

- the essential characteristics of a lease
- the difference between a lease and a licence
- enforceability of leasehold covenants
- rules for passing of the benefit and burden of leasehold covenants
- privity of contract and privity of estate
- remedies for breach of leasehold covenants
- purpose and effect of an alienation covenant
- the ways in which a lease can be terminated.

■ WHAT DO YOU KNOW ALREADY?

Try answering these questions before reading this chapter. If you find some difficult or cannot remember the answers, make a note to look more closely at that subtopic during your revision.

1) True or false? The landlord of a leasehold estate will *always* be the owner of the freehold estate from which the lease has been granted? **[The leasehold estate, page 94]**

2) A client owns a block of flats which has four separate flats. The client sells flat one and two then rents flats three and four to separate families for a term of one year, but it can automatically renew until either party gives notice to vacate. Which of the following best represents the legal status of these separate occupiers?

   a) The client is the owner of the entire freehold estate in land and landlord of flats one, two, three and four.

   b) The client is the owner of the entire freehold estate in land and landlord of flats one and two. The owners of flats three and four are the legal estate holders of the lease.

   c) The client is the owner of the entire freehold estate in land and landlord of flats three and four. The owners of flats one and two are the legal estate holders of the lease.

   d) The client is the owner of the entire freehold estate in land and landlord of flats one, two, three and four. The occupiers of flats one and two are the leasehold legal estate holders and the occupiers of flats three and four are tenants under a periodic tenancy.

   e) The client is the owner of the entire freehold estate in land and landlord of flats one, two, three and four. The occupiers of flats one and two are the leasehold legal estate holders and the occupiers of flats three and four are tenants under fixed term lease.

   [Registration, page 96]

3) True or false? Privity of estate refers to the people who are the original parties to the lease. They are the only ones who can sue or be sued following any breach of the clauses in that lease. **[Rules for passing the benefit and burden of leasehold covenants, page 103]**

4) A landlord granted a lease in December 1999. He is now selling his freehold reversion and wishes to be released from any future liability under the lease. How much notice does he have to give to the current tenant to ask to be released from his liability in this way?

   a) four weeks

   b) eight weeks

c) two weeks

d) There is no time frame, he will be automatically released when he sells the freehold reversion and the liability will pass to the new owner of the freehold estate.

e) There is no time frame and he will never be released from this liability as the lease was granted post 1996.

[Rules for passing the benefit and burden of leasehold covenants, page 103]

5) True or false? A landlord can apply to terminate a lease by way of surrender?

[Ending a lease, page 111]

THE LEASEHOLD ESTATE

We briefly touched upon the concept of the leasehold estate in **Chapter 4** but before we can begin to understand how a lease operates, it is important to be aware of the current definition of a lease and some key terms that you will need to be aware of as you work through this chapter.

The Law of Property Act 1925 provides us with a very brief definition of a **leasehold estate**, that being 'a term of years absolute'. It then goes onto provide a long-winded and confusing explanation of this definition, which may explain the scope of case law in existence when determining if a lease has been created.

Key term: leasehold estate

You may find that the leasehold estate is called 'lease', 'leasehold', 'demise' or 'term of years absolute', which all mean the same thing in the context of leases. This is the legal estate and one of the two legal estates recognised by law.

A **landlord** creates the leasehold estate out of the freehold estate and assigns this lease to the **tenant**. This will be for a fixed term and the landlord will retain the legal interest in the freehold estate, otherwise known as the *freehold reversion*. It is also important to note that there can be several leases granted over the same piece of land and if it is not prevented by an *alienation covenant* within the lease, a tenant is able to **sublease** the land.

Key term: landlord

Another term for landlord is the 'lessor'. This is the person who has created the leasehold estate out of their freehold estate (in some instances they may also be referred to as the freeholder).

Key term: tenant

Another term for tenant is the 'lessee'. This is the person who has been granted the lease.

Key term: sublease

A further assignment of the existing leasehold estate to a third party. This must be for a term shorter in duration than the original lease (which would then be known as the head-lease).

Figure 5.1 shows how a lease can be created in more detail.

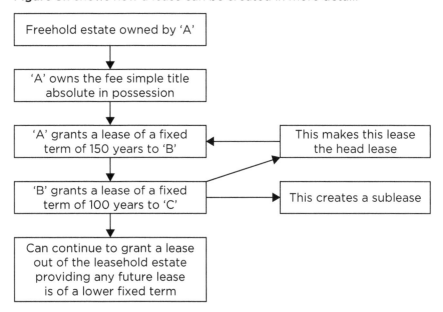

Figure 5.1: The creation of a lease

Types of lease

It is also worth briefly considering the different types of lease that can be created. Those are:

- fixed term lease, which is usually the most common and the one that this chapter will focus on. This type of lease *cannot* last indefinitely, there must be an agreed maximum term at the start of the agreement.

• periodic tenancy, a lease which *may* last indefinitely. It could run from week to week, month to month. The tenancy keeps being renewed at the end of the agreed term and is only ended when either the landlord or the tenant gives notice to the other.

Registration

Another brief, but important consideration for the creation of a lease is whether it needs to be registered to be valid.

A legal lease must be created by a deed, whether it needs to be registered will depend on the duration of the lease. Some leases do not need to be registered and they take effect as an overriding interest instead. This was considered in detail in **Chapter 2**.

The Land Registry only require leases of over seven years duration to be registered to be a legal estate in land. Most leases of up to seven years can be legal leases provided the necessary formal requirements have been met as they would take effect as an overriding interest. The flowchart at **Figure 5.2** shows the requirements for these different leases.

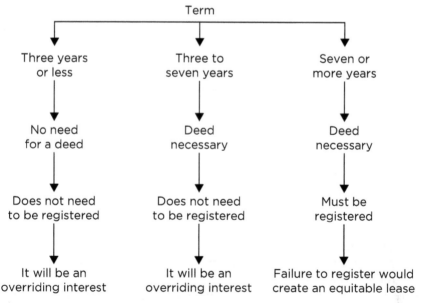

Figure 5.2: Registration of leases

Practice example 5.1 will show how these initial principles could work in a practical scenario.

Practice example 5.1

Julie has purchased a piece of land which is freehold. She builds two houses on the land and she sells each house with the benefit of a 150-year lease. Olivia purchases one of the houses and moves in. Harper purchases the other house but decides not to move in and wishes to let the property to some students. She grants the students a tenancy for one year. What legal interest does each party have in this land?

- Julie retains the freehold legal interest in the land. She has the superior 'freehold reversion'. (She is both the freeholder and the landlord under the lease.)
- Olivia and Harper both have a legal interest in their respective properties. They own the leasehold interest. Whilst they would have to surrender the leasehold estate at the end of the 150-year term, that is unlikely going to concern them during their lifetime. During their ownership they can sell the legal interest to a third party or carry out any other registrable disposition. (Chapter 4 considers this in detail.)
- The tenants will have a periodic tenancy. Their occupation of the land is with the agreement of Harper. They do not have a legal interest in the leasehold or freehold estate. At the end of the one-year term they would have to vacate the property if given notice by Harper to do so.

We will now consider the essential characteristics of a lease and how to distinguish this from a licence.

ESSENTIAL CHARACTERISTICS OF A LEASE

Now you have the basic concept of how a lease is created we need to consider what the courts have determined to be the essential characteristics of a lease. The landmark case of *Street v Mountford* [1985] provided three key characteristics of this 'term of years absolute' which were as follows:
- exclusive possession
- a fixed duration
- at a rent. However, the courts have since decided that this final requirement is no longer necessary and so we will not be exploring this further.

A further characteristic introduced by the Law of Property (Miscellaneous Provisions) Act 1989, is that the lease must have the correct formalities to be a valid legal lease, such as being made by a deed and being signed. If the lease is not made with the correct formalities then the tenant may only hold an equitable lease and not a legal lease. These differences were considered in **Chapter 2**.

Exclusive possession

This means that the tenant has the right to control the use of the property. They can decide who goes into the property and they can exclude anyone from the property, even the landlord.

It is important to contrast this with a **licence**, which merely grants the occupier permission to stay in the property and does not grant them any legal or proprietary interest in the land. A licensee may be permitted exclusive occupation of the property, but unless they have exclusive possession they will not hold a lease.

Key term: licence
Is a personal right permitting someone to occupy land for a fixed term? They do not obtain any proprietary rights in the land and must vacate the land at the end of the term.

It is important to distinguish between a lease and a licence as a tenant under a lease has additional statutory protection, such as from the Rent Act 1977, which provides a mechanism for the tenant to ask a court whether the rent being charged is fair.

Practice example 5.2 may help to show the differences between a lease and a licence.

Practice example 5.2
Emil owns a house and enters into a written agreement with Darcie. The terms of the agreement are that she would pay £37 rent per week and the agreement could be terminated within 14 days. Emil has called the agreement a 'licence agreement'. Emil does not provide any additional services for Darcie as part of her occupation. He does not have spare keys for the property and Darcie is able to permanently exclude him from the property. Darcie applied to the court to get the rent assessed and as a result Emil applies to the

court for a declaration that Darcie only holds a licence and so has no statutory protection. Does Darcie hold a lease or a licence?

These are the facts of *Street v Mountford* [1985], from which this requirement of 'actual occupation' for a lease was founded. The court were not concerned with what the document was called, what was necessary was to look at the actions of the parties and the rights created. The found that the actions of the parties meant there was a lease in place and not a licence.

Exam warning

You may receive a question stating that a client has a document called a 'licence'. It does not matter what the document is called, what matters is the rights conferred on the client. If they have obtained exclusive possession then they will have a lease and the document being called a licence may simply be a sham.

A fixed duration

The second essential characteristic of a lease is that it must be for a fixed term, which means it is fixed for a maximum duration. There is no minimum or maximum term permitted, but it must not exceed the landlord's own term. The flowchart in **Figure 5.1** explained this in more detail, and landlord B could not grant any lease with a longer term than his own lease of 150 years.

Leases will usually contain forfeiture clauses allowing for the lease to be terminated earlier than the agreed fixed term, which we will explore later in this chapter.

This can be compared to a typical lease of a room in shared accommodation by a student. Whilst the tenancy agreement is likely to say it is for a period of six months, there is also likely to be an agreement that the tenancy can continue on a month-by-month basis automatically and will only come to an end once the landlord or tenant has given the appropriate notice. This is a type of periodic tenancy and again shows the differences you need to look out for to determine if you are dealing with the creation of a legal lease.

The flow chart shown in **Figure 5.3** may provide a helpful reminder of these essential characteristics.

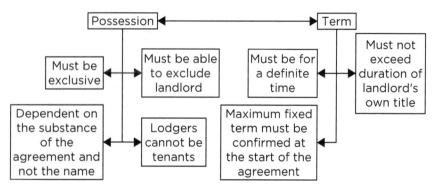

Figure 5.3: Essential characteristics of a lease

LEASEHOLD COVENANTS

You will see that this has been separated out from freehold covenants (**Chapter 7**) as there are some distinct rules which apply to covenants of leasehold land. This section of this chapter will consider the following, all of which fall under this broad heading of leasehold covenants:

• privity of contract and privity of estate
• enforceability of leasehold covenants
• rules for passing the benefit and burden of leasehold covenants
• remedies for breach of leasehold covenants
• purpose and effect of an alienation covenant.

Key term: covenant

A lease can contain many different **covenants**, which are effectively promises between the landlord and tenant that they will either do something on the land or that they will not do something.

Covenants will be separated in the lease between the covenants that must be carried out by the landlord or carried out by the tenant. These leasehold covenants can either be express covenants contained in the lease (the deed) or they can be implied covenants under statutory provisions.

Revision tip

As this chapter specifically considers the requirements for a legal lease, when referring to the landlord we will always be referring to the person who has created the lease out of their legal estate (whether that be a superior leasehold or freehold). The tenant will always be the person who has acquired a legal estate in land, being the leasehold estate. We will not cover the position of a tenant who has not acquired that legal interest in land, such as a tenant on a periodic tenancy.

Express covenants

As you would expect, these are written into the lease and will be determined by what the landlord feels appropriate. These could include covenants preventing animals being kept in the property or covenants preventing any alterations to the property without the landlord's prior consent.

Implied covenants

Implied covenants will be deemed to be included into every lease unless there is a specific clause stating that it will not apply. We shall separate these into the covenants implied onto the landlord and those implied onto the tenant.

Landlord implied covenants

These include:

- quiet enjoyment. This means that the landlord must allow the tenant to enjoy the occupation of the property without interference from the landlord from the date the tenancy starts. There will be no implied covenants for the breach of quiet enjoyment for issues that may be in existence before the start of the tenancy.
- non-derogation from grant. Meaning that if the tenancy is granted for a specific purpose then the landlord cannot do anything to undermine that during the term of the lease.
- repair. The repair obligations will depend on the type of lease. In leases where the tenant owns the leasehold estate, there is likely to be repair obligations expressly stated in the lease, or they may be divided between the landlord and tenant.

Practice example 5.3 will consider these landlord implied covenants in more detail.

Practice example 5.3

Tony is the owner of a freehold estate in land. He owns a house on the land and builds a second house in the grounds. He grants a lease of the house for a term of 100 years, which he then sells to Grace.

One of the terms before Grace purchased the leasehold estate was that she could grow and then sell fruit and vegetables on the land. To do this, all customers would need access over Tony's land by way of a small footpath at the rear of his garden, but Grace agreed to pay for the maintenance and repair of the footpath. These conditions were not contained in the lease. Tony then builds a two-storey barn on the boundary line which blocks all direct sunlight to the land. He also prevents customers from buying her produce by blocking the pathway. Could any of these provisions be implied into the lease?

They possibly could. Preventing the direct sunlight needed to grow these crops and then also preventing customers from accessing the land could be seen as a breach of quiet enjoyment as Tony appears to be substantially interfering with her lawful enjoyment of the property. It could also be a breach of non-derogation from grant. Tony agreed that Grace could use the land for a specific purpose, but his conduct is then preventing her from doing that. Finally, it is perfectly possible for the repair obligation to fall upon Grace if that is what she agrees to in the lease, but it would not be implied in this way against her. If she has agreed to pay for the maintenance then Tony would be required to maintain the footpath.

Within long leases it is very common to see shared obligations for repair. The landlord may be required to continue to maintain and repair any commonly used areas, such as stairways in a block of flats; however, the tenant is likely to be required to pay some money on a monthly basis for the maintenance to be carried out as the tenant is the one using the common areas.

Tenant implied covenants
These include:
- paying rent and taxes. Whilst there doesn't need to be rent for a lease to exist, if it does then there will be an implied covenant that the tenant will pay it. However, these provisions are usually expressly stated in the lease.
- repairing. As mentioned in **Practice example 5.3**, repair obligations are not usually implied upon a tenant. However, again there is likely to be an express clause stating that the tenant will keep the property in good repair and condition. Everyday wear and tear will be expected but the tenant should not do anything on the land that could significantly reduce the value of the landlord's land.

* not committing waste. This does not mean 'waste' in the conventional sense; it means that the tenant cannot do anything on the land which would permanently change the landlord's land.

Practice example 5.4 will consider these tenant implied covenants in more detail.

Practice example 5.4

Using the same scenario from **Practice example 5.3**, we know that Tony is the owner of a freehold estate in land and he has granted a lease of a house on the land for a term of 100 years, which he has sold to Grace. One of the terms is that Grace would pay a ground rent of £20 per month, payable directly to Tony. This term is contained within the lease. Grace has never paid this ground rent in the 12 months that she has owned the leasehold estate. Grace has also planted an invasive species of weed on her land which has spread onto Tony's land and caused damage to the foundations of his property. He has been advised that it will likely cost in the region of £10,000 to correct these problems. Would Grace be in breach of any implied provisions?

She possibly could be in breach of some of these implied provisions. She is clearly in breach of the obligation to pay her rent. This is both an express and an implied condition. If she has knowingly brought the invasive weed onto the land then she could be in breach of both the repair and the waste obligation as she has done something on the land which has permanently changed the landlord's land.

Whether these covenants are enforceable will depend on who owns the land at that present time and whether the lease was granted pre- or post-1996.

Rules for passing the benefit and burden of leasehold covenants

There are different rules depending on whether the land is in the ownership of the original landlord or tenant (privity of contract), or whether the land has been sold or transferred to a third party, a successor in title (privity of estate).

Between original landlord and tenant

The covenants in a lease are essentially clauses in a contract between the landlord and tenant and, quite simply, **privity of contract** will apply where there is a breach of one of those conditions throughout the duration of the lease.

If there is a breach by either party of any of the covenants between the original landlord and tenant then the other can bring proceedings to try and remedy the breach. We shall consider remedies later in this chapter.

> **Key term: privity of contract**
>
> Only those who are parties to the contract can sue or be sued following any breach of the clauses in that contract.

So, privity of contract will only apply to the original parties to the lease for the time they are in legal ownership of the estate in land. We shall now consider the position of the enforcement of covenants between successors in title of both the freehold and leasehold estates, both pre- and post-1996.

Between successors in title of the freehold estate: pre-1996

An initial point to remember is that both the landlord (usually the owner of the freehold estate in land) and the tenant (the owner of the leasehold estate in land) can sell their legal interests at any time, so the owner of the leasehold estate in land, which has 99 years remaining on the lease, can sell that whole legal estate to another person. That person will then take over the remaining term and so on.

Whilst the original parties of the lease are bound by privity of contract, successors in title will be bound by **privity of estate**, which refers to the nature of the relationship between the landlord and the tenant. Both the landlord and the tenant have their own estate in that piece of land and so privity of estate only looks at who currently has that estate in land and who must, at that particular time, comply with those covenants.

> **Key term: privity of estate**
>
> This refers to the rights and duties that apply between the current owners of the different legal estates in the same piece of land.

For leases granted before 1996 the successors in title would not be bound by every covenant in the original contract (lease). Only those covenants which 'touch and concern' the land will be enforceable between them.

Figure 5.4 shows how these obligations can change between the different parties.

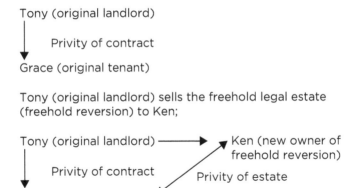

Tony (original landlord)

Privity of contract

Grace (original tenant)

Tony (original landlord) sells the freehold legal estate (freehold reversion) to Ken;

Tony (original landlord) ──────► Ken (new owner of
                                        freehold reversion)
Privity of contract   Privity of estate

Grace (original tenant)

Figure 5.4: Privity of contract and privity of estate

This introduces the privity of estate between Ken, the new owner of the freehold legal estate, and Grace. There is no privity of contract between Grace and Ken as Ken is not the original party to the contract – that relationship remains between Tony and Grace only.

The difficulty that arises here is that the original landlord, Tony, still remains liable to Grace for any breach of covenant by Ken. In order to protect himself, Tony would have to obtain an indemnity from Ken that he would repay Tony for any of the costs if he was sued for any breach carried out by Ken. **Practice example 5.6** shows this in practice.

Practice example 5.6

Ken has breached a covenant to keep the drains in good repair. There has been a blockage which has caused damage to Grace's property. Ken has no money to fix the drains and is filing for bankruptcy. Who would be liable for the cost of this repair?

Ultimately, this would fall to Tony. If Ken does not or cannot pay, then Grace can sue Tony as the original landlord. He would then need to try and recover the expenses from Ken. If unsuccessful then he will bear this cost.

Between successors in title of the freehold estate: post-1996

The main difference introduced with the 1995 legislation is that it ultimately removes that ongoing liability from the original landlord, providing they write to the tenant asking to be released from that liability. If the tenant agrees, or does not reply within four weeks, the landlord will be released from that ongoing obligation. **Practice example 5.7** shows this in more detail.

Practice example 5.7

Before Tony sold his freehold reversion to Ken he wrote to Grace asking to be released from any ongoing liabilities. She did not respond within the four-week timescale. Ken breached a covenant to keep the drains in good repair, causing a blockage which has caused damage to Grace's property. Ken has no money to fix the drains and is filing for bankruptcy. Who would be liable for the cost of this repair?

Ultimately, this would now fall to Grace. She would have to sue Ken to resolve this issue as Tony has no further liability under the lease.

We will now consider the rules of enforcement between the original and new owners of the leasehold estate.

Between successors in title of the leasehold estate: pre-1996

We will now consider how the covenants can be enforced if Grace sells her leasehold estate in land to Austin. **Figure 5.5** shows how these obligations continue to change between the different parties.

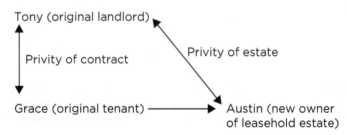

Figure 5.5: Privity of contract and privity of estate

This works exactly the same as for the sale of the freehold estate. If Austin does not comply with one of his covenants, say to pay his ground rent, then Tony could sue Austin directly as there is the privity of estate between them. If he still doesn't pay he could look to recover the costs from Grace as there is still privity of contract between them.

Between successors in title of the leasehold estate: post-1996

Again, as with the freehold reversion, the main difference introduced with the 1995 legislation is that it removes that ongoing liability for the original tenant. However, in this case the tenant does not have to write to ask to have their liability removed and it is automatically assumed; meaning that Grace would no longer have any liability under the lease as soon as she has assigned the lease to Austin.

Exam warning

If you are faced with a question of where the ownership of the freehold and leasehold estates is now with successors in title it would be wise to remember that any personal covenants between the original owners will no longer be enforceable between the successors in title. For example, if Grace had covenanted with Tony to provide him with a weekly basket of fresh vegetables from her allotment, that would cease to be enforceable once they have both sold their legal interests.

Figure 5.6 shows the enforceability of covenants.

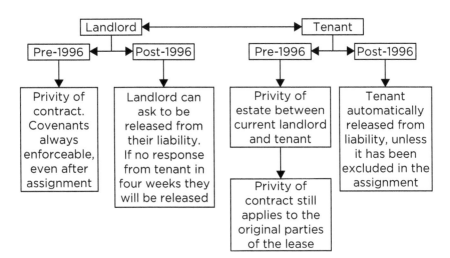

Figure 5.6: Enforceability of covenants

One final point to consider in the enforceability of covenants is that of **alienation covenants**.

Alienation covenants

The main purpose of an alienation covenant is to prevent a tenant from assigning, subletting or parting with possession of the property. However, it is also common to have a further condition stating that permission to assign, sublet or part with possession of the property should not be unreasonably withheld.

Revision tip

These types of alienation covenants are more commonly associated with the leasehold estate owners in a large block of flats or commercial premises as the landlords like to keep track of who is living in the properties, usually for insurance purposes.

This type of covenant would not stop a tenant from assigning or subletting in this way but this is still a breach of a covenant in the lease, which would mean that the landlord can seek a remedy to rectify the breach. This could possibly mean that the person who has agreed to sublet the property may lose their right to do so.

Key term: alienation covenant

A clause in a lease preventing the assignment or sublet of a property.

Now we have considered how someone can be liable under the lease, we need to consider what remedies may be available for the party who is not at fault.

REMEDIES

Whilst this is something that would fall under the usual contractual remedies, it is important that you are aware of what remedies are available to each party for a breach of covenant in a lease.

Remedies available to the landlord

- action for debt/damages: this would be in the usual way of claiming any damages or debt by making an application to the small claims court.

- an injunction: this would be a court order stopping the tenant from continuing with the breach. For example, if there is a covenant specifying that the tenant cannot build any extension without the landlord's consent, but they go ahead with the work anyway, the landlord could seek an injunction to stop that work.
- specific performance: this would require the tenant to specifically carry out something which they have not done; for example, if the tenant was required to repair the fences and they do not. Whilst this is still a remedy available to a landlord, the courts are very reluctant to use it and prefer to make an order for damages instead.
- forfeiture: this is one of the more drastic remedies available to a landlord and effectively allows the landlord to terminate the lease and take control of the leasehold estate as they will have the 'right to re-enter' the property.

As this is such a draconian measure, it is heavily regulated by statute and there are also a number of reliefs to the remedy available to the tenant. Different rules apply to forfeiture if this action is taken due to non-payment of rent or any other breach and so we will consider those in turn.

Forfeiture for non-payment of rent
To use this remedy the landlord must:
- make a formal demand for the outstanding rent, unless there is express exemption of this in the lease or the rent is in arrears by six months or more
- ensure there is a forfeiture clause in the lease.

If these terms are satisfied the landlord can then either re-enter the property forcefully or apply to the county court for possession proceedings.

A tenant may however be given relief from forfeiture if:
- they can pay the outstanding rent within five days of the hearing.

The court also has the power to stop the proceedings for four or more weeks. If the tenant pays the arrears in full they will be granted automatic relief from forfeiture.

Forfeiture for any other breach of covenant

To use this remedy:
• there must be a forfeiture clause in the lease
• the landlord must consider whether the breach is remediable.

If it is remediable then the landlord must serve a notice specifying the time limit in which to remedy the breach. If the breach is remedied then the right to forfeiture is lost. If it is not remedied then the application can proceed to the court for forfeiture.

If the breach is not remediable then the landlord must still serve a notice specifying this, but must then wait 14 days before making an application to the court for forfeiture.

Again, a tenant may be given relief from forfeiture if:
• they can show the court that they have remedied the breach or
• they can persuade the court that the lease should continue even though there has been a breach. This will of course be very subjective on the individual facts of the case.

Remedies available to the tenant

• Damages: this would be in the usual way of claiming any damages or debt by making an application to the small claims court.
• Injunction: this would be a court order stopping the landlord from continuing with or carrying out an anticipated breach.
• Specific performance: this would require the landlord to specifically carry out something which they have not done.
• Recoup the costs of repairs from future rent: if the landlord has not carried out repairs, and the tenant has given a notice on the landlord specifying the repairs. The tenant could then withhold future rent to repay the costs of those repairs.

Exam warning

Caution should be taken if you need to advise a tenant on remedies available to them in the exam. For example, while they could look to recoup the cost from future rent, they need to ensure the correct notice procedure has been carried out as the landlord can of course then claim forfeiture for non-payment of rent if this has not been carried out correctly.

Figure 5.7 shows all the remedies available to a landlord or tenant.

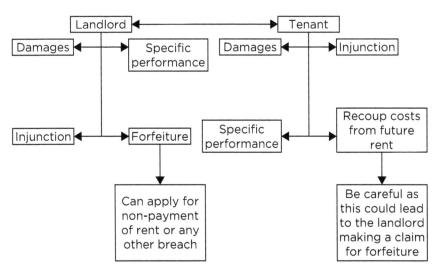

Figure 5.7: Remedies available for breach of covenant

Finally, you will need to know the ways in which a lease can be terminated.

ENDING A LEASE

There are a number of ways that a lease can be ended. These are:

- expiration: this would happen if the lease came to the end of the agreed fixed term. For example, if a lease has been granted for 12 years, at the end of those 12 years the tenant will lose the right to that legal estate and it will revert back to the freehold estate owner. This is, however, very rare and most leasehold estate owners will either apply to extend the lease or purchase the freehold reversion, but that is outside the scope of this revision guide.
- forfeiture: as considered in the remedies section, forfeiture would also bring the legal lease to an end.
- surrender: again, quite simply, the leaseholder may decide they no longer wish to be in ownership of the leasehold estate and decide to give this back to the freeholder. This must be completed by a deed to ensure there is full consent given by the leaseholder to this.
- merger: finally, the leaseholder could apply to purchase the freehold reversion. If that happens they can apply to merge the freehold and leasehold legal titles. Again, this is outside the scope of this revision guide.

■ KEY POINT CHECKLIST

This chapter has covered the following key knowledge points. You can use these to structure your revision around, making sure to recall the key details for each point, as covered in this chapter.

• The starting point when considering a leasehold estate is that it is created out of a freehold estate. Meaning, you have those two legal estates, freehold and leasehold, in one piece of land.

• This chapter focuses on the legal relationships between the estate owners, so the legal owner of the freehold estate and the legal owner of the leasehold estate. This is quite different to the status of someone who is simply renting property that does not legally belong to them.

• Different types of leases have different requirements for making them a legal lease. A lease of less than seven years does need to be registered to be legal, it can be an overriding interest on the registered estate. Leases of over seven years must be registered to be legal. They cannot be overriding and failure to register would create an equitable lease.

• The essential characteristics of a lease are that they are of a fixed duration and that the owner has exclusive possession. This is necessary to understand the differences between a lease and a licence. A tenant who has a lease has additional statutory protections.

• It does not matter if a document is called a lease or a licence. If you are trying to show that a client has a lease, then what matters is that the essential characteristics of a lease are proven and determining what rights are conferred on the client.

• Leasehold covenants can be very complex when determining who is liable for any breach of them.

• This can be split into four broad categories; leases created before 1996, leases created after 1996, if the breach is between the original parties to the lease or whether the breach is between successors in title. Careful consideration needs to be given to assess those details before deciding whether a specific party is liable for a breach of covenant.

• Both the landlord and the tenant under a lease can be subject to covenants. These can be expressly written into the lease or they can be implied.

• Alienation covenants are very common in all types of lease. These will prevent a tenant giving away possession of the property, such as sub-letting to a new tenant. Breach of an alienation covenant could result in the new occupier losing occupation.

- There are a number of remedies available to both the landlord and the tenant for breach of covenant. Most commonly these would be the standard contractual remedies available to all, such as suing for debt or damages. Injunctions are common with landlords to prevent a tenant from continuing to breach a covenant and non-payment of future rent can be common with tenants, but caution must be exercised if recommending this course of action as that could allow the landlord to make a claim for forfeiture for non-payment of rent.
- A lease can come to an end at the end of the fixed term, or by agreement from the tenant. This would need to be evidenced by a deed to show the tenant has consented. The lease can also be forfeited if there is a breach of covenant.

■ KEY TERMS AND CONCEPTS

- leasehold estate (**page 94**)
- landlord (**page 94**)
- tenant (**page 94**)
- sublease (**page 94**)
- licence (**page 98**)
- covenant (**page 100**)
- privity of contract (**page 103**)
- privity of estate (**page 104**)
- alienation covenant (**page 108**)

■ SQE1-STYLE QUESTIONS

QUESTION 1

A client is renting a room in a shared house. She shares the house with four other friends, each having their own bedroom, and commonly shared rooms, such as the kitchen. The original agreement between the client and the landlord stated that she could rent the room for one year. It has now been four years and she has never had a new agreement. The landlord has never visited the property and the client is not sure if the landlord has keys. The client is up to date with her rent but the landlord has recently told her he is selling the house and given her and her friends notice to vacate the property. The client is unhappy with this and would like to know if she can stay. A friend has told her she may have a legal lease.

Which of the following is the best description of the client's legal position?

A. If the client can demonstrate that she has exclusive possession, then she could make a claim for a legal lease to remain in the property.

B. If the client can demonstrate that she has exclusive possession and the agreement is for a fixed term, then she could make a claim for a legal lease to remain in the property.

C. The client does not have exclusive possession as she shares the house with four friends and will not have a legal lease.

D. The landlord should have renewed the agreement with the client each year. Failure to do so will mean the client can make a claim for a legal lease to remain in the property.

E. The client does not have exclusive possession and the agreement did not stipulate a definite maximum term. This does not meet the requirements of a legal lease.

QUESTION 2

A client would like to grant a new lease of a house located on his farmland. The house has been on the land for many years. The client wants to keep the landlord obligations to a 'minimum' but is happy to include a clause granting quiet enjoyment to the tenant. The client sells the property and sometime later seeks advice on a complaint that the tenant has made. The tenant of the house is claiming that the client is in breach of the quiet enjoyment covenant as the noise of the animals and machinery coming from the farm is constantly disturbing the tenant. The tenant claims that the walls of the house are not soundproofed and wants the landlord to correct this immediately.

Which of the following best represents the correct legal position of the client?

A. If there is anything which is causing substantial interference with the tenant's lawful enjoyment of the land then the client is in breach of the express clause for quiet enjoyment.

B. If there is anything which is causing substantial interference with the tenant's lawful enjoyment of the land, which was existing before the lease was granted, then the client is not in breach of the express clause for quiet enjoyment.

C. If there is anything which is causing substantial interference with the tenant's lawful enjoyment of the land, the client is in breach of the implied clause for non-derogation from grant.

D. If there is anything which is causing substantial interference with the tenant's lawful enjoyment of the land, which took effect at the point the lease was granted, then the client is not in breach of the express clause for quiet enjoyment.

E. If there is anything which is causing substantial interference with the tenant's lawful enjoyment of the land then the client is in breach of the express clause for non-derogation from grant.

QUESTION 3

A client has sought advice as she is being sued for breach of covenant in a lease. The client owned the leasehold estate in land for five years and then sold this to the new owner last month. The original landlord still owns the freehold estate in land and he has written to her complaining that she has breached a covenant that she had agreed to when the lease was granted. The covenant was: 'to cut the grass on the garden area belonging to the landlord at least once a month during the months of March to October'. The client has not cut the grass as she no longer lives there.

Which of the following is the best advice to give to the client?

A. The client is in breach of this covenant as it is personal in nature and so it is forever enforceable under the privity of contract.

B. The client is not in breach of this covenant but the new owner is. All covenants remain enforceable after the original tenant has sold the land.

C. The client is in breach of this covenant as it touches and concerns the land and so is forever enforceable under the privity of contract.

D. The client is not in breach of this covenant and neither is the new owner. This is no longer enforceable under the privity of estate.

E. The client is in breach of this covenant as it is personal in nature and so it is forever enforceable under the privity of estate.

QUESTION 4

A client has sought advice as her landlord has continually failed to repair a leak in the roof of the communal areas of a block of flats. This is causing flooding in the stairwells and is extremely dangerous as the stairs are slippery. The client pays a small rent of £30 per annum under the terms of the lease, but there is an express covenant saying that the landlord is responsible for the upkeep of these communal areas.

Which of the following is the best advice to give to this client?

A. The client and all other flat owners should stop paying the rent immediately. They can then pool that money together to fix the roof and recoup the costs from the landlord by non-payment of future rent.

B. Only the client should stop paying the rent immediately. She would then have to pay to have the roof fixed but continue to recoup the costs from the landlord by non-payment of future rent.

C. The client could stop paying the rent due to the landlord's failure to fix the roof, but she must give him notice of the issue and give him reasonable time to repair the same before she fixes it herself. The client must ensure the correct procedure is followed or she may find that the landlord makes a claim for forfeiture for non-payment of rent.

D. The client is only able to make a claim to the court for specific performance to make the landlord fix the roof. There are no other remedies available to her for breach of a repair covenant.

E. The client could stop paying the rent due to the landlord's failure to fix the roof, but she must give him notice of the issue and give him reasonable time to repair the same before she fixes it herself.

QUESTION 5

A client has sought advice on a demand for payment that she has recently received. The client was the owner of a freehold estate in land and she granted a lease of a house located on the freehold land in 1994. The term of the lease was 125 years. The client then sold her freehold estate to a new landlord in 1998. She has since received a letter from the original tenant under the lease demanding payment for damage caused to her house, which has arisen by the failure of the current landlord to maintain the land, which is an express covenant in the lease. The tenant claims that the current landlord is bankrupt and cannot afford to pay for the repairs and under the terms of the lease she can seek repayment from the original landlord.

Which of the following best reflects the correct legal advice?

A. The client is no longer liable for any breach of covenant on the lease and all liability passed to the new landlord on completion of the sale.

B. The client is no longer liable for any breach of covenant on the lease as the sale took place post-1996. As such, all liability passed to the new landlord on completion of the sale.

C. The client is liable as the lease was created pre-1996. Privity of contract still exists between the original landlord and the original tenant and so the covenants can be enforced for the duration of the lease term.

D. The client is liable as the lease was created post-1996. Privity of contract still exists between the original landlord and the original tenant and so the covenants can be enforced for the duration of the lease term.

E. The client is no longer liable for any breach of covenant in the lease and the tenant would need to sue the current landlord in the usual way to claim damages.

■ ANSWERS TO QUESTIONS

Answers to 'What do you know already?' questions at the start of the chapter

1) The correct answer was false. The landlord is not *always* the owner of the freehold estate from which the lease has been granted. If there is a sublease then the landlord will be the owner of the leasehold estate from which that sublease has been granted.

2) The correct answer was D. If the client is the owner of the entire land and then grants individual leases from that land then the client would be considered the landlord and the owner of the superior freehold title, the freehold reversion. This means that the client is still the landlord whether a long lease of a fixed term has been granted and the legal estate in that land sold to a new owner, as with flats one and two, or whether a shorter lease has been granted for the mere occupation of the land as with flats three and four. The owners of flats one and two are the legal estate owners of those flats and so they can sell or carry out any other registrable disposition on that land. The occupiers of flats three and four are occupiers under a tenancy agreement, meaning they would have to vacate the land if

asked to do so by the landlord. We know it is a periodic tenancy as the question states it can continue indefinitely and so there is no fixed term.

3) The correct answer was false. The description given in the question refers to the relationship you would find under privity of contract. Privity of estate looks at the relationship between the landlord and tenant in existence at that particular time.

4) The correct answer was A, four weeks. E is incorrect as a landlord only retains liability for leases granted pre-1996 not post-1996.

5) The correct answer was false. Surrender is only available to the tenant (leasehold estate owner) as they must consent to this by way of a deed. The landlord (usually the freehold estate owner) cannot apply for this.

Answers to end-of-chapter SQE1-style questions

Question 1:

The correct answer was E. This is because there are two main requirements to determine if you have a legal lease. Those are that it must grant the client exclusive possession, meaning that she must be able to exclude the landlord completely. There must also be a definite fixed term agreed from the start, and this must be an agreed maximum period, which can then be ended sooner if necessary. A, B and C are incorrect as whilst she may have exclusive possession, she does not have a definite fixed term. D is incorrect as there is no need to renew the lease each year if it continues on a week by week or month by month basis.

Question 2:

The correct answer was B. Here we are considering either the express or implied covenant for quiet enjoyment. We know that the landlord has expressly included this in the lease and so we do not need to be concerned with answer C which talks about implied covenants. Likewise, we do not need to be concerned about answer E which make reference to non-derogation from grant as that is not applicable here. Option B is correct as it talks about interference which was existing *before* the lease was granted. These covenants are prospective, meaning they only take effect from the moment they are granted. The problems arising from a lack of soundproofing would have been in existence for many years before the lease was granted. Option D is incorrect as it is worded incorrectly. It states that the landlord would not be in breach of the covenant for anything which starts at the point the lease is made, which is incorrect as the landlord could possibly be in breach in that situation. A is incorrect as it is too broad and makes reference to any interference, which is incorrect as it only applies from the date the lease is granted.

Question 3:

The correct answer was D. This is a clear example of a covenant which is for the personal benefit of the original landlord. As the original tenant has sold her leasehold estate she is no longer bound by this covenant. The new leasehold estate owner does not need to comply with this covenant as it does not 'touch and concern' the land. Under the privity of contract only those covenants which are not personal in nature will be binding on the new estate owner. This is why the other answers can be disregarded. A, B and E are incorrect as personal covenants are not forever enforceable, definitely not to new owners. C is incorrect as personal covenants do not 'touch and concern the land'.

Question 4:

The correct answer was C. The client can stop paying a rent, even if it is a low rent like this one. If there is an express covenant for repair obligations then breach of that can be dealt with in one of three ways; an application for damages to the court if she pays for the repair herself; however, there is no guarantee she will be successful in that, or she could apply for specific performance to order the landlord to fix the same, or she could pay to fix the roof and stop paying future rent, but she must take caution when doing so and ensure she follows the correct procedures so she is not at risk of finding herself subject to court proceedings for forfeiture due to non-payment of rent, which is why E is incorrect as it does not include this additional information. A is incorrect as whilst the client could ask all of the other flat owners to chip in, that answer does not go far enough in warning the client of the consequences of doing so, which is why that is not the best answer. B is incorrect as it does not talk about giving the landlord prior notice, which she must do. D is incorrect as she has other remedies and this type of breach is not limited to specific performance.

Question 5:

The correct answer was C. You are told that the lease was created in 1994 and so you need to consider the pre-1996 rules. These clearly state that the original parties to the lease enjoy privity of contract; they are the original parties to the lease and so the covenants are enforceable between them for the duration of the lease. B and D are incorrect as they talk of the lease being created post 1996, which it was not and the question states it was created in 1994. A and E are incorrect as the lease was created pre-1996 and so there remains privity of contract between the original parties to the lease.

■ KEY CASES, RULES, STATUTES AND INSTRUMENTS

The SQE1 Assessment Specification does not require you to know any case names, or statutory materials, for the topic of land law.

6

Easements

This chapter will focus on the key elements of easements, which are specific types of property right allowing somebody to use land owned by another person. This will usually be for a specific purpose, such as the right for one neighbour to cross over land owned by an adjoining neighbour to access a garage.

Easements can arise in several ways. This chapter will focus on the legal requirements that need to be met to determine whether there is an easement in existence and how to acquire or dispose of easements, including whether they are enforceable against future owners. This chapter will break down a typical easement scenario and explain how to approach this step by step.

Without these rights it would be impossible to operate a successful system of land law in England and Wales as land would simply become overburdened, abandoned or landlocked.

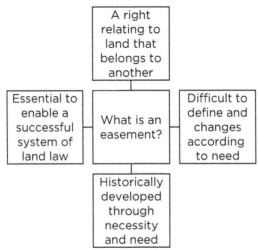

■ SQE ASSESSMENT ADVICE

As you work through this chapter, remember to pay particular attention in your revision to:
- easements as proprietary rights in land
- the essential characteristics of easements
- the different methods for creating easements.

■ WHAT DO YOU KNOW ALREADY?

Try answering these questions before reading this chapter. If you find some difficult or can't remember the answers, make a note to look more closely at that subtopic during your revision.

1) Which of the following rights cannot be an easement?
   a) the right of the owners of one house to use a neighbour's kitchen for the purposes of washing their clothes
   b) the right to use a swimming pool or tennis court on adjoining land
   c) the right of the owners of one building to be protected from the weather by an adjoining building
   d) the right to use a shed on a landlord's adjoining land for the storage of coal
   e) the right to cross neighbouring land to access a nearby road
   [What is an easement?, page 123]

2) True or false? The decision in *Re Ellenborough Park* deals with the requirements needed for a right to be an equitable easement.
   [The creation of easements, page 135]

3) For an easement to be granted by necessity which of the following must be proven?
   a) It was always the understanding of both parties that the easement would be used.
   b) The land is completely unusable without the easement.
   c) There has been continuous use of the easement for more than 20 years.
   d) It is required for the reasonable enjoyment of the property.
   e) It was verbally agreed between the two respective landowners.
   [The creation of easements, page 135]

4) When a legal easement is created by express grant there must be:
   a) a verbal agreement
   b) a written agreement

c) a deed

d) use of the land for over 20 years

e) common intention between the parties

[**The creation of easements, page 135**]

5) True or false? The rule in *Wheeldon v. Burrows* deals with the creation of easements by prescription.

[**Implied grant or implied reservation, page 137**]

WHAT IS AN EASEMENT?

An **easement** is the right to cross or otherwise use someone else's land for a specific purpose. Whilst this may sound simple enough, there is no list of all of the different rights that could be an easement and this can make identification difficult at times.

Key term: easement
A right to cross or otherwise use someone else's land for a specific purpose.

Before we consider how to establish whether a specific right can be an easement, it may be helpful to initially consider what type of rights could be classed as an easement. These could be:

• rights of way, such as on foot or by vehicle over a neighbouring property
• rights to water through a pipe which crosses over neighbouring land
• right of support from an adjoining building
• right to hang a sign on another's property
• right to enter neighbouring land to repair your own property
• right to use a swimming pool or other recreational facilities.

The fact that we cannot succinctly define what rights could be classed easements will go some way to explaining the issues that can be encountered when dealing with a question on easements and why it is important to approach any question in the specific order that we will consider in this chapter.

Revision tip
Easements are very different to a public right of way, which can be used by anybody. Easements exist to prevent the land from being overburdened which is why the use of an easement is only available to those who have some connection to the land.

HOW TO ESTABLISH AN EASEMENT

The first consideration is to work out whether the right to use land owned by somebody else qualifies as an easement. There are several important steps that you must work through:

1) Firstly, does the right qualify as an easement?
   - To answer this, you must consider the criteria in *Re Ellenborough Park*, which is discussed later in this chapter.
2) If the right is a valid easement, has it been validly created?
   - An easement can only be created expressly (by deed) or by implication. Again, the method of creation of the easement will be discussed later in this chapter.

There are several additional matters to consider when working through these two initial steps which we will examine in turn below.

Does the right qualify as an easement?

Look at **Practice example 6.1** and think about whether this right is capable of being an easement.

Practice example 6.1

James and Alma were the original owners of buildings and land which surrounded a large, grassed area. The surrounding land was sold off in separate plots and each deed granted the purchasers the right to use the central grassed area. Houses were built on the surrounding land, and the owners exercised their right to use the grassed area. This central grassed area was then sold, and the new owners intended to build upon it. The owners of the surrounding houses claimed the right to use the land and to prevent the building. Can the owners of the surrounding houses claim they have a valid easement over the grassed area?

These are the facts of *Re Ellenborough Park* [1956]. The Court of Appeal upheld the claims and the right to use the grassed area, or 'the park' could exist as a legal easement.

In *Re Ellenborough Park*, the judges set out the defining essential characteristics of an easement, which are:

a) there must be a **dominant** and a **servient tenement**
b) an easement must accommodate the dominant tenement
c) dominant and servient owners must be different people
d) the right claimed must be capable of forming the subject matter of a grant.

Key term: dominant tenement

A piece of land which is benefited by some third party right.

Key term: servient tenement

A piece of land which bears the burden of some third party right.

It is important that you have a clear understanding on each of these elements and we will work through these in turn below.

There must be a dominant and servient tenement

The key feature here is that there must be a particular *piece of land* which obtains a benefit from the easement and another piece of land which grants that benefit. Look at **Practice example 6.2** which explains this further.

Practice example 6.2

Clara must use her neighbour's drive to access her property. As Clara is the one using the land, she is the owner of the 'dominant tenement' and as her neighbour's land is being used by Clara, this is the 'servient tenement' as shown in **Figure 6.1**.

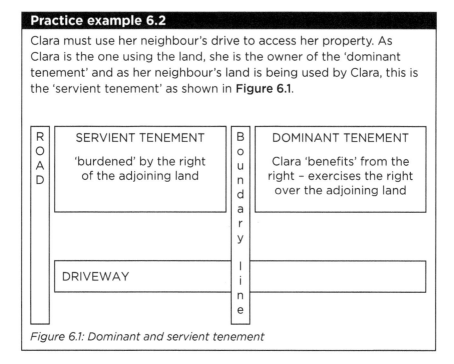

Figure 6.1: Dominant and servient tenement

Revision tip

Map out a small plan, as in **Figure 6.1**, when tackling any problem-based question relating to easements. This should allow you to have a clear idea of which is the dominant tenement and which is the servient tenement. This could also give you some insight into *how* the easement has been created (ie, necessity etc, which will be explained further in this chapter).

Once you have clearly established that there is a separate dominant and servient owner, then you can move on to the second principle from *Re Ellenborough Park,* and that is that the easement must accommodate the dominant tenement.

The easement must accommodate the dominant tenement

The right claimed must benefit the *land* itself and not just the owner of the land personally. Looking at **Figure 6.1** again, if Clara had another way of accessing the house but she simply wanted to use the private road as it was more convenient for her, then it would be a personal benefit and not a benefit to the land.

It can be difficult to clearly distinguish between a personal benefit and a benefit for the land and this is something that students can sometimes struggle with. Consider **Practice example 6.3** below which explains this further.

Practice example 6.3

Ash had been granted a lease of land next to a canal, together with an exclusive right to hire out boats on the canal. Ash then claimed that she had a right to the sole use of the canal based on an easement. She claimed that the servient 'land' was the canal and the dominant land was a small part of the bank where she sold tickets and arranged the hiring of the boats. Do you agree that the use of the canal was a benefit to this small piece of land on the bank of the canal? Or was it simply a benefit to Ash personally?

These are the facts of *Hill v Tupper* [1863] where the court refused the application for an easement because the right did not accommodate the dominant tenement and it was merely a personal right granted under the lease. It benefited the business and not the land. Ash would not have been successful in her claim as her use of the canal benefited her personally, not the land next to the canal which she leased.

This shows that it can be difficult to clearly distinguish between a personal benefit and a benefit conferred on land and the question of 'accommodation' has been determined by case law as follows:

- The easement is not dependent upon *specific characteristics or identity of the owner of the dominant tenement,* as can be shown in **Practice example 6.4**.
- The two pieces of land *should be close in proximity, although not necessarily adjacent.* It would clearly be beneficial for you to have a right of way over adjoining neighbouring land, but no such benefit would exist for someone who lived 100 miles away.
- The easement cannot be *purely recreational* in nature, which is becoming more relaxed following recent case law and is considered in **Practice example 6.5**.

Practice example 6.4

Bobby lives at number 1 Elm Drive. He allows his children to play on an area of wasteland directly next to his house. Bobby then moves to number 2 Elm Drive, which is a house across the street and Jane moves into number 1. Bobby's children continue to play on the wasteland. Can this benefit Jane as the new owner of number 1?

No, it will only act as a purely personal benefit to Bobby and so it cannot form the subject matter of an easement. An easement which states 'to allow Bobby's children the right to play on the land' does not benefit Jane nor is it for the benefit of the house.

Land for purely recreational use?

Historically, it was considered that easements cannot be *'purely recreational'*. However, that has changed in recent years. Take a look at **Practice example 6.5** which highlights the changes to this category of easements.

Practice example 6.5

Twenty-four time-share villas are situated opposite Broome Park, which is a large property that provides different leisure and sporting facilities. These facilities were open to members of the public who paid to use them. In 1981, the villa owners had been granted, by deed, the right to use 'the swimming pool, golf course, squash courts, tennis courts, the ground and basement floor of Broome Park, the gardens and any other sporting or recreational facilities ...'

The owners of Broome Park now want the villa owners to pay for these recreational facilities, stating that the right did not run with the land or bind successive owners. Do you agree that the use of these recreational facilities is for the benefit of the land or the benefit of the owners of the time-share villas?

These are the facts in the recent Supreme Court case of *Regency Villas Title Ltd v Diamond Resorts (Europe) Ltd* [2018] in which the Court determined that the right to use the swimming pool, golf course, tennis courts, squash courts, putting green and croquet lawn were valid easements and made it clear that in modern times physical exercise is regarded as essential or desirable and can take many forms. They also agreed that such easements could be granted providing it did not require the servient owner to spend money on maintaining the facilities.

Exam warning

Accommodation of an easement is clearly going to be a question of fact. It is very clear that the issues of 'value' and benefit to the dominant tenement, are going to vary along with changing social demands and accepted modes of property use. There can be a risk of thinking only about the benefit to the dominant owner and not to the land.

One way to consider this is: does the right claimed increase the value of the land or its saleability? If yes, then it is likely going to be sufficient to demonstrate that it accommodates the land, rather than just the dominant owner. Be mindful of this if you need to consider this for your SQE1 examination.

You must now consider the third principle from *Re Ellenborough Park*, and that is that the dominant and servient owners must be separate and different people.

The dominant and servient owners must be different people

This is one of the simpler conditions to clarify and merely requires assessing whether the two pieces of land are separately *owned and occupied* (have another look at **Figure 6.1** to see this demonstrated).

The simple reason for this is that a landowner who owns both the dominant and servient land has no need for an easement. They can use and pass over their own land as they see fit and they cannot exercise the right against themselves. This is particularly important when considering the rule from *Wheeldon v Burrows* which we will consider later in the chapter.

It is, however, important to note that it is possible for a tenant to have an easement over the landlord's property; for example, a tenant of a flat will usually have a right of way over the landlord's property to reach their front door, so whilst the landlord may own both pieces of land, they are occupied by different people at the relevant time.

The final principle from *Re Ellenborough Park* is that the right must be capable of being the subject matter of a grant, or more simply, being defined in a deed.

The right claimed must be capable of forming the subject matter of a grant

This is crucial to the nature of easements. In essence it means that the easement 'must be capable of being granted by a deed'. If you think of the essential elements of a deed as explained in **Chapter 1**, then this should be easier to follow and apply. This element can be broken down into three key components:

1) The easement must be defined clearly and free from ambiguity.
2) There must be someone who is capable of granting the easement (grantor) and someone who the easement can be granted to (grantee).
3) It must be like existing forms of easements, so nothing new or novel that has not been granted previously.

Let's look at these separate factors in turn.

The easement must be defined clearly and free from ambiguity

The right claimed must be clear enough to be described in a deed. This is probably best explained by considering situations where there has not been sufficient definition of the right claimed, such as a right to a view, which was held to be too vague.

Exam warning

This is one of the elements that students do struggle with. If this comes up in the assessment, try and consider the issue or a right being 'definable' as to *specify distinctly* the right you are claiming. Could you, for example, claim a right for children to play on a piece of land? Could you write this down and describe it if you were drafting a deed? How will you define this? What exactly can they do on that land? Are there certain parts of the land this is limited to? Compare this to children playing in a park: this is much easier to define in a deed.

There must be someone who is capable of granting the easement and someone whom the easement can be granted to
This is a straightforward element to satisfy:

• a *grantor*: in essence, the easement must be granted by someone who has the power to do so; for example, a statutory corporation with no power to grant easements would not satisfy this element but the owner of a freehold piece of land who wanted to grant his neighbour access over his garden, would.

• a *grantee*: there must be a suitable defined person(s) who the easement can be granted to. For example, it is not possible to grant an easement to an undefined body of persons such as 'all of the nurses at the QE Hospital'.

In most cases the grantor and grantee will be obvious and they are usually adjoining neighbours.

It must be like existing forms of easements
Again, this is a provision which has evolved with case law and it is accepted that the following factors must be considered when dealing with this requirement:

a) Exercise caution when considering 'novel rights' and no new negative easements.
b) It must not be too extensive (known as the 'ouster' principle).
c) It must be no positive burden on the servient owner.

We will consider these further factors in turn.

Exercise caution when considering 'novel rights'
Whilst the courts are willing to consider new easements based on our changing social requirements (see **Practice example 6.5**) and the list of easements is certainly not a closed one, the courts are conscious

of preventing new 'novel' rights that will bind successive owners. Read **Practice example 6.6** and consider whether this is a novel right being claimed.

Practice example 6.6

A large commercial building has been built close to Christine's house and due to the size of the new building her television signal is now very poor. Christine and her neighbours are all experiencing the same issue and want to bring a claim against the owners of the new building on the basis that they had an easement for uninterrupted television signals to their homes. Based on everything you have read so far, do you agree that this is capable of being a valid easement?

These are the facts in *Hunter v Canary Wharf* [1997] and the court refused the claim and said that an easement for uninterrupted television signals was too vague and uncertain, especially as there were several people benefiting from it and they could not all be specifically identified. It was also held that it would interfere too much with the servient land.

One matter the courts have made clear is that they will not recognise any new **negative easements** because of the restrictive impact they would have on the neighbouring land.

Key term: negative easement

A negative easement is a right which is enjoyed without any action required by the dominant owner. There are several established forms of negative easements such as:
• rights of support, preventing an adjoining neighbour from removing existing structures
• rights of light, preventing an adjoining neighbour from building on their land which may prevent the light to the neighbouring land.

Compare this with a positive easement, where the dominant owner must take action to exercise the right, such as actually walking or driving over the servient land.

Attempt to answer **Practice example 6.7**; would you consider this to be an easement?

Practice example 6.7

The owner of servient land demolished his house completely, which left a wall of the dominant land exposed to the weather. The dominant landowner claimed an easement for the right of protection from the weather. Can you have an easement for 'protection from the weather'?

These are the facts from *Phipps v Pears* [1965] in which the Court of Appeal refused on the basis that this would restrict the servient owner and hamper the development of the property. They felt the dominant owner could have protected his property by seeking an agreement with the adjoining neighbour not to demolish a wall, which could have then been binding on any subsequent owners as a restrictive covenant (see Chapter 7).

It must not be too extensive (the 'ouster' principle)

The second point to consider is that the easement only has a *limited* right or use of another's land. An easement is a right to 'use' the land, not a right to 'possess' the land.

This issue is mostly seen in easements of storage and parking and whilst it seems a relatively simple requirement, the courts have sometimes struggled to find the 'line' where 'use of land' tips into 'possession of land'.

Exam warning

You may need to consider a scenario on whether parking of a car or storage on servient land is an easement. The important thing to remember is that too much or 'over possession' of land belonging to another could amount to a claim which is considerably greater than that which is conferred by an easement, such as a lease. It is possible to have an easement of storage or parking on neighbouring land but the key point is that this will be accepted as an easement if the dominant owner does not store too much or completely deprive the landowner of control of that land.

Table 6.1 sets out several different cases that have considered issues with storage This is just to illustrate how the ouster principle has been applied if required in the SQE exam, and you do not need to memorise the names.

Table 6.1: Key cases on storage

Case name	Facts
Wright v Macadam **[1949]**	A tenant could have a right to store coal in her landlord's shed.
Copeland v Greenhalf **[1952]**	The court refused to accept that an easement had arisen for a wheelwright to park his wagons, wheels and other vehicles on a strip of land belonging to the servient landowner. The court felt this conferred too great a power on the dominant owner and the claim really amounted to a claim for joint occupation of that strip of land.
Grigsby v Melville **[1972]**	The parties were owners of adjoining properties and the defendant was claiming a right to store coal in the cellar beneath the neighbour's house. The judge indicated that he would have followed the decision in *Copeland v Greenhalf*, since in his view the right claimed amounted to excessive use of the cellar.

Similar difficulties have been faced by the courts in easements of parking; **Table 6.2** below sets out several examples so you can see how the principle has been applied.

Table 6.2: Key cases on parking

Case name	Facts
London & Blenheim Estates Ltd v Ladbrooke Retail Parks Ltd **[1992]**	The court suggested that the test is one of degree and that the 'line' would be crossed when the right is so extensive that it would amount to occupation of the land and leave the servient owner with no reasonable enjoyment of their land. If, however, there is room for the dominant tenant to park their car and other uses, then an easement of parking could exist.
Batchelor v Marlow **[2003]**	The court held that parking six cars on the servient land between the hours of 8.30am and 6.00pm rendered the servient owners' use of the land erroneous and without any reasonable use of their land, for parking or otherwise. This decision seemed to introduce the 'substantial interference' test.

Key cases on parking (continued)

Case name	Facts
Moncrieff v Jamieson [2007]	The parking took up the entirety of the relevant space. The space in question was one of necessity for the dominant owner as their house was perched on the edge of a cliff and there was nowhere else to park the car.
	Lord Scott suggested that the test should not focus on the area of the parking space relative to the whole of the servient land, but instead should focus upon whether the servient owner retains sufficient possession and control over the part of the land of which the right is claimed.

So, as you can see there is no specific rule on what would amount to excessive use and it must be based on fact and degree in each case. Do try to remember that if it arises in your SQE1 exam questions.

It must be no positive burden on the servient owner

The final point to consider when ensuring the easement is like existing forms of easements is that, generally, the servient owner must not be obliged to do anything or spend money as a result of the grant of the easement. The only thing the servient owner must do is allow the dominant owner to exercise their right without interference. This can be seen in **Practice example 6.8**.

Practice example 6.8

Marcus has an easement to run electricity cables over his neighbour's land. The electricity supplier has refused to connect the supply unless the neighbour also grants the electricity supplier a direct easement. Would requiring the neighbour to enter into a direct easement with a third party, unrelated to the land, meet the requirements of a valid easement?

No, it would not, and these are the facts of *William Old International Ltd v Arya* [2009] and the court held that a servient landowner had no obligation to do this. An easement cannot oblige the servient landowner to enter into a contract or proprietary relationship with a third party (and likely cost them money in legal fees).

If you can satisfy all these requirements then you can be sure that the right claimed is *capable* of being an easement. The flow chart shown in **Figure 6.2** may help you to work through these steps.

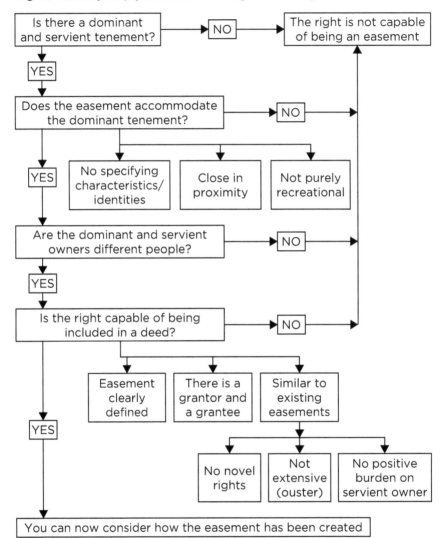

Figure 6.2: Does the right qualify as an easement

THE CREATION OF EASEMENTS

You will need to have a firm grasp of the ways in which easements can be created as part of your SQE1 revision.

There are four main ways in which easements can be created:
- expressly
- impliedly
- by prescription
- by statute.

To help you work through this chapter, **Figure 6.3** gives an overview of these which we will then look at in detail.

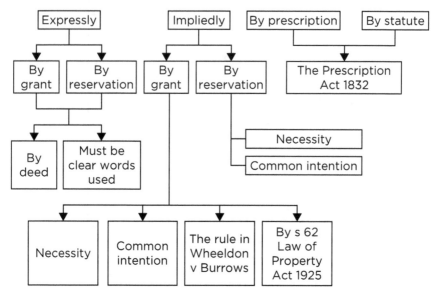

Figure 6.3: Four principal modes of creating an easement

Express grant or express reservation

Express grant or reservation is possibly the most straightforward and the most frequently encountered mode of creating easements. Firstly, it may help to revise what is meant by **express grant** or **express reservation**.

Key terms: express grant or express reservation

Clara owns a property and sells part of it to Jim. He wants to be able to use part of Clara's drive to access his land. She will *grant* him the right to do so in the legal deed. However, Clara also wants to continue to be able to use the part of the driveway on Jim's land; she will *reserve* herself the right to do so, also in the deed.

The definitions above seem simple but this is something that can be confusing and could possibly mean answering a question incorrectly if these two terms are interpreted the wrong way. **Figure 6.4** below may help when revising this.

Here Clara is selling plot A, but she still needs to use the driveway which crosses through plot A to access her property. She should 'reserve' herself an easement to do so in the deed.

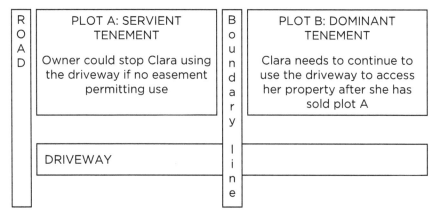

Figure 6.4: The dominant and servient tenement

For both an express grant and an express reservation, appropriate words must be included into the deed transferring title to the land from the servient owner to the dominant owner. The grant must be made by a deed and whilst there is no specific form of words that must be used, clarity of the drafting is particularly important to avoid any disputes in the future.

Implied grant or implied reservation

The implied grant or reservation of an easement is created in a situation where there are no express words (grant or reserve) in any legal document, but it is still an easement that can be 'read' into the legal document.

Implied grant

Firstly, we will consider how easements can be *impliedly granted* into a deed. Remember, to grant an easement means that an owner of a plot of land will grant a specific right over their land for the benefit of another, usually adjoining land.

There are four ways in which an easement can be impliedly granted which are:
• by *necessity*
• by *common intention*
• under *the rule in Wheeldon v Burrows*
• by *operation of s 62 LPA 1925.*

We shall look at these in turn.

Grant by necessity or common intention
Firstly, we will consider reservation into the deed by 'necessity'.

• *grant by necessity*

This is very straightforward and applies if the land would be *completely* landlocked without the easement being granted and as such is *'necessary'*, for the use of the land. This is prevalent in respect to two types of rights:
• rights of support, eg, if Beth owns adjoining terraced houses and then sells one she would not want the new owner to start removing adjoining walls. Beth could claim an easement of support has been impliedly granted by necessity
• rights of way, eg, Beth owns adjoining terraced houses and the only way to access her front door is to cross through the neighbouring garden. She sells one house and again would not want the new owner to prevent her access. She could claim an easement of a right of way has been impliedly granted by necessity.

The courts are very strict in determining necessity and have determined that the land must be completely inaccessible. The justification of this type of easement is to keep land usable. **Practice example 6.9** demonstrates this further.

Practice example 6.9

Diren builds a new house for himself on his existing garden and then sells the original house. In doing so he leaves no way to access the public highway. He would need to pass over the land he previously owned to access the highway. The new owner is refusing to allow this. Can Diren obtain the necessary easement?

The likely answer is yes. The access over the previously owned land is necessary for the use of the new house. It is landlocked without it.

If, however, there was another way of accessing the land, even if that means was not quite so convenient, there would be no reservation of an easement by necessity.

• *grant by common intention*

The second way an easement could be impliedly inserted into a deed is by common intention. This could be classified as those easements which are not strictly *'necessary'* for the use of the land, but which were commonly intended between the parties for that use of the land. For one reason or another (usually an oversight) the easement was not included in the deed. Look at **Practice example 6.10** which explains this further.

Practice example 6.10

Emma and Florence have been neighbours for several years. They both own a semi-detached house and the boundary line of the properties runs down the middle of a shared pathway. The pathway is only three foot wide but is used by both Emma and Florence to gain access to their respective gardens. A dispute has arisen between them over who is allowed to use the path. The deed is silent on this issue. Has an easement by common intention been impliedly granted into the deed?

This is based on the facts of *Kent v Kavanagh* where the court agreed that due to the fact the path was only three feet wide, it would not be possible for one owner to access their garden without crossing over onto the adjoining neighbour's land. The legal document must have intended that the path would have been used in this way and it would always be the common intention of the owners to do so.

Grant of easement under the rule in Wheeldon v Burrows

The third way easements can be *impliedly granted* into a deed is under the rule established in the case of *Wheeldon v Burrows*. The *only* situation you would find this is where a landowner sells part of their land to someone else. The transfer would impliedly contain *all* the rights of enjoyment that the original landowner enjoyed. This is demonstrated further in **Practice example 6.11**.

Practice example 6.11

Myrella owns a large plot of land, which is split into plots A and B. During her ownership she used a path on the land which leads directly to a public woodland. Myrella sells plot B and retains plot A for herself. The transfer deed does not expressly create an easement allowing the owner of plot B to continue to use the path. Could the new owner of plot B make a claim for an easement under this rule?

The simple answer is yes, they could. This is demonstrated further in Figure 6.5.

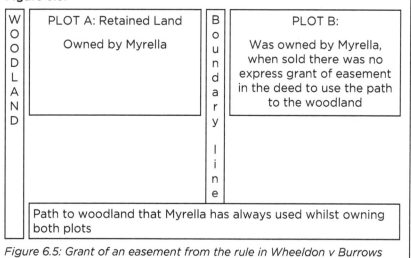

Figure 6.5: Grant of an easement from the rule in Wheeldon v Burrows

---

The main purpose of this provision is to *imply* into any conveyance the grant of all **quasi-easements** that had been exercised by the seller prior to the transfer.

Key term: quasi-easements

This is the use of land which would have become an easement if the land in question had not been in the full ownership of one person. It is impossible to grant yourself a right of way over land that you own – it is unnecessary.

Only certain rights are capable of being easements under this rule and they must meet the following criteria:
• There is a quasi-easement.
• The right was in use immediately prior to the transfer of the land.

- The right must be continuous and apparent (so the use is obvious).
- The right is necessary for the reasonable enjoyment of the property.

Revision tip

What you need to remember for your revision is that *'necessary'* is not the same as the elements of *'necessity'* – the latter of course meaning that the land is completely unusable without the right being granted.

Practice example 6.12 considers these additional conditions further.

Practice example 6.12

George held an equitable lease (see **Chapter 5**) of a house for seven years. He used a driveway that ran over the landlord's property during his time in occupation. There was a separate access way to the property (and as such necessity could not apply here). The landlord tried to stop George from using the drive. Can the landlord do this?

These are the facts of *Borman v Griffith* and the court held that he was entitled to use the drive as it was 'plainly visible' and it was 'necessary for the reasonable enjoyment of the property'. The landlord had used the drive and the two parcels of land had been in the landlord's common ownership at one time. The easement was implied using the rule from *Wheeldon v Burrows*.

Exam warning

The rule of *Wheeldon v Burrows* can be daunting when first introduced to it but if you are faced with a question like this then keep in mind that this particular rule will only apply where a party is selling or leasing part of their own land, and they *themselves exercised* that right when they owned all of that land. It also only applies to the *grant* of new easements, not reservation by the original landowner.

Grant of easement under s 62 LPA 1925

The final way in which easements can be impliedly *granted* into a deed is under s 62 LPA 1925. This statutory provision essentially upgrades a licence that had been granted by the owner of land to the tenant, to an easement when the land is subsequently sold or the lease is renewed.

It could be interpreted as a 'word saving' provision to save parties having to expressly set out in the deed any physical features forming part of the land and so certain easements and rights are deemed to be automatically included in any new legal deed.

It has received a rather wide interpretation by the courts and it can create new easements in favour of a purchaser, as well as transferring those that already exist. **Practice example 6.13** shows how this might apply to a SQE question.

Practice example 6.13

Asrah has a tenancy agreement for two rooms that she rents from her landlord, Nadine. Nadine had given Asrah permission to use a shed at the bottom of the garden to store some possessions. Asrah renewed her tenancy and took on a new tenancy of another room; the new tenancy agreement contained no reference to use of the shed. Asrah continued to use the shed until Nadine asked her to start paying for it but Asrah refused. Has an easement been created here when the new tenancy agreement was signed?

Yes, the original licence to use the shed for storage had been converted to an easement of storage by s 62 LPA when the new tenancy agreement was signed.

There are several rules that apply when considering this method:

- There must be a conveyance of land (some form of deed of the legal estate).
- The right claimed must be capable of being an easement, as set out in *Re Ellenborough Park*.
- The conveyance must not express a contrary intention between the parties (such as excluding s 62).
- There must be diversity of occupation, meaning the two pieces of land must be in separate ownership, unlike the rule in *Wheeldon* which required common ownership of the land before the transfer.
- Recent case law has also introduced a new provision of the right being 'continuous and apparent'.

These provisions can be shown in **Practice example 6.14**.

Practice example 6.14

A plot of land was split and then sold in two plots. Plot 2 had several tracks and bridleways crossing over it into plot 1, which were used by the owner of plot 1. Plot 1 was then sold and the new owner carried out extensive works and regularly crossed over plot 2 to gain access to plot 1. The owner of plot 2 then erected a gate to prevent the access from continuing. The owners of plot 1 made a claim for an easement. Would this be successful under s 62 LPA?

These were the facts of _Wood v Waddington_ [2015] and the owner of plot 1 was entitled to the right of way under s 62. The rights were 'continuous and apparent' and sufficient evidence of use was present. Use of the track once a month was held to be sufficient to show this.

Implied reservation

Now, we will consider how easements can be impliedly _reserved_ into a deed. Remember, to reserve an easement is to allow the original landowner continued access over the land they are selling, after they have sold it. There are only two ways in which this can occur:

• reservation by _necessity_ and
• reservation by _common intention._

It is important to be aware that there is a higher burden of proof on a seller of a piece of land claiming an implied reservation of an easement, but the principle of _'non derogation from grant'_ will be considered by the courts. Look at **Practice example 6.15** below to consider how this could be applied to a SQE1 question.

Practice example 6.15

Maaz owns two flats. Each flat has its own access, but there are services that are used commonly with the other flat, such as drainage and chimneys. Maaz sells one of the flats to Brandon but continues to live in the other flat. Maaz then blocks the chimney and prevents Brandon from using it. Can Maaz do this?

These are similar facts to those seen in _Jones v Pritchard_ [1908]. The court used the principle of 'non derogation from grant' which means a person cannot grant something and then hold back rights that would make the grant useful, such as selling a house and then not allowing the owner to use a chimney.

Firstly, we will consider reservation into the deed by 'necessity'.

Reservation by necessity

This is very straightforward and applies in the same way as a grant by necessity explored earlier in this chapter. It applies if the land would

be completely landlocked without the easement being reserved and as such is *'necessary'*, for the use of the land. This is prevalent in respect to two types of rights:
• rights of support and
• rights of way.

Again, the courts are very strict in determining necessity and the land must be *completely inaccessible.* Look at **practice example 6.16** which demonstrates this further.

Practice example 6.16

Jameila builds a new house for herself on her existing garden land and then sells the original house, but in doing so she leaves no means to access the public highway and there is no other access to the new plot. She needs to pass over the land she previously owned to access the highway. The new owner is refusing to allow this. Can Jameila obtain the necessary easement?

The likely answer is yes. The access over the previously owned land is necessary for the use of the land. It is landlocked without it.

Reservation by common intention

The second way an easement could be impliedly reserved into a deed is by common intention. This could be classified as those easements which are not strictly *'necessary'* for the use of the land, but which were commonly intended between the parties for that use of the land. For one reason or another (usually an oversight) the easements were not included in the legal deed. Look at **Practice example 6.17** which explains this further.

Practice example 6.17

A block of four terraced houses were owned by Charles. All houses have a path to the rear of the gardens which allows all owners to pass over to access their bins. Charles sells off three of the houses but when he sold the end house he forgot to reserve a right of way over the back garden and along the side of the other houses. The path was visible on the plan and had been used by all four houses on the terrace. Would this fall under a 'common intention' reservation?

These are the facts of *Peckham v Ellison* [2000] and whilst the court accepted that it was harder to demonstrate a reservation of

an easement, they held that the burden had been discharged and there was a common intention to reserve that right of way.

Grant of easement by prescription

The creation of easements by prescription means they can be acquired by the long use of the easement, and the Prescription Act 1832 provides for prescription under two different time periods:

- 20 years: if the easement has been enjoyed without interruption for 20 years and does not depend on one of the conditions set out below.
- 40 years: if the easement has been enjoyed without interruption for 40 years then it will be deemed 'absolute and indefeasible', even if the easement was based on an oral agreement.

Where there has been *at least* 20 years' use, there are three basic rules which apply. Those are:

- The user must be 'as of right' which encompasses:
  - 'without force', so no physical force from the other landowner and no objections
  - 'without secrecy', so the use must have been open and honest
  - 'without permission', meaning that the use must not be in reliance upon some permission, such as a licence or the payment of a fee.
- The use must be by a freehold owner against another freehold owner; you cannot claim prescriptive rights over a landlord or third party – it must be freehold land.
- The use must be continuous.

Look at **Practice example 6.18** to explore this further.

Practice example 6.18

You have been instructed by James, who has used a path that runs along the rear of his neighbour's property for over 20 years. He has accessed this at least once a month in that time. The neighbouring property has been sold, and the new neighbour has now put a locked gate on the entrance to the path. Can James make a claim to the court for an easement by prescription?

Answer: yes, he could. You would still need to consider all the initial elements of *Re Ellenborough Park*, but you could then skip straight to 'grant by prescription'. He can demonstrate 20 years continuous use, which has been without force, without secrecy and without permission.

■ KEY POINT CHECKLIST

This chapter has covered the following key knowledge points. You can use these to structure your revision around, making sure you recall the key details for each point, as covered in this chapter.

- Easements are important property rights owned by one landowner (the dominant tenement) over land of another (the servient tenement).
- To exist, an easement *must* meet the requirements of *Re Ellenborough Park*; being that there is a dominant and servient tenement, the easement must *accommodate* the dominant tenement, the dominant and servient owners must be different people and the easement must be capable of being described in a deed.
- Accommodation of the easement can be difficult to satisfy, but the emphasis must be on the benefit to the land in question and not to the person.
- To satisfy the requirements of a deed the easement must be clear, defined and capable of certainty; there must be a capable grantor and grantee and it must be similar to existing forms of easements.
- Caution needs to be exercised if you have a question that considers 'novel rights', ie, those that are unusual and have never been held to be easement before; there can never be any new negative easements, so always consider the wording and impact on the servient landowner. Do they need to spend money, or take some direct action to fulfil the easement? If so, it is likely to be a negative easement.
- To be a valid easement it cannot be too extensive (also known as the 'ouster' principle) and there must be no positive burden on the servient owner; the only requirement from them is that they allow the dominant owner the access they have granted.
- Once you have satisfied all requirements to show that you have a valid easement, you then need to go on to consider how the easement has been created, which can be by statute, deed, implication or prescription.
- Easements can be expressly granted or reserved, which is the simplest method of creating an easement providing there is a deed and there are clear words used to specify what the easement is.
- Easements can be impliedly reserved by necessity or common intention. Impliedly means that there is nothing in writing, or no express creation, but there is evidence in place of the easement and so it can be 'written' into a deed.
- Easements can be impliedly granted by necessity, common intention, only under the rule in *Wheeldon v Burrows* or by s 62 LPA 1925.
- Easements can be acquired by long use under the PA 1832.

■ KEY TERMS AND CONCEPTS

- easement (**page 123**)
- dominant tenement (**page 124**)
- servient tenement (**page 124**)
- negative easement (**page 131**)
- express grant and express reservation (**page 136**)
- quasi-easement (**page 140**)

■ SQE1-STYLE QUESTIONS

QUESTION 1

A client has recently purchased a house and shortly after moving in he noticed his neighbour walking across his garden. When confronted, the neighbour informed the client that she must cross over his garden to access the park and that she has done so for over 25 years. The path is clearly visible. The only other means of accessing the park is to walk over a busy road which takes her twice as long. The client puts up a gate to prevent the neighbour from accessing his land and he has now been informed that she has made an application to the court for an easement by necessity.

Which of the following best represents the legal position?

A. The neighbour's claim will be successful as she has no other means of safely accessing the park.

B. The neighbour's claim will fail as she cannot prove that there has previously been a quasi-easement.

C. The neighbour's claim will be successful as she can prove that it was the common intention of the parties for her to use this path.

D. The neighbour's claim will fail under necessity but likely be successful if the application was made by prescription.

E. The neighbour's claim will be successful. She has demonstrated that the land is completely landlocked.

QUESTION 2

A client has decided to sell a small piece of land from his very large farmland. The client will require vehicular access over the piece of land he is selling to attend to crops in an adjacent field. He has always accessed his crops in this way during his 30-year ownership of the farm.

Which of the following best represents the advice this client should be given?

A. The client can continue to access the land as the easement will be implied by necessity.

B. The client can continue to use the land as the easement will be implied by common intention.

C. The client can continue to access the land if it is written into the deed as an express grant of an easement.

D. The client can continue to use the land on the basis that he is granting an easement over part of his own land, and he exercised that same right when he owned all of that land.

E. The client can continue to access the land if it is written into the deed as an express reservation of an easement.

QUESTION 3

A client owns two plots of land. He sold plot A and retained plot B, where he still lives now. The client agreed with the new owner of plot A that he would reserve himself a right to use a footpath to the rear garden of plot A and this was contained in the deed. Ownership of plot A has changed again and the new owner is refusing to let the client use the footpath, stating that the only way the client can use the footpath is if the new neighbour expressly grants him an easement, which he is refusing to do.

Which of the following best represents the correct legal position?

A. The neighbour is correct. A legal easement can only bind a future successor in title if the original grantor enters a new deed every time the land is sold.

B. The neighbour is incorrect. Legal easements bind the world and if registered on the title deeds then this will be binding on every successor in title.

C. The neighbour is correct. It is only the owner of servient land who can grant an easement over it when the land is sold.

D. The neighbour is incorrect. There is clear and continued use and so the easement would be impliedly reserved into any future deed.

E. The neighbour is correct. However, he could not grant the easement and it would need to be the owner of the dominant land to grant an easement over servient land.

QUESTION 4

A client owns two flats in the same building, one above the other. Each flat has its own access, but there are services that are in common use with the other flat, such as drainage and chimneys. The client sells one flat and remains living in the other. She then stops the other flat owner from using the chimney by blocking it.

Which of the following best represents the legal position?

A. This is an example of a quasi-easement and the neighbour will be able to make a claim for the easement to continue using the chimney.

B. This is an example of a reservation of an easement by prescription due to long use.

C. This is an example of a reservation of an easement by common intention.

D. The client is entitled to stop any common services if she no longer needs use of the same. Providing her access is not blocked then there is no legal issue and the other neighbour would need to arrange a different means of using the chimney.

E. This is an example of 'non derogation from grant' which means a person cannot grant something and then hold back rights that would make the grant useful.

QUESTION 5

A client has recently purchased a house and has encountered several difficulties with the neighbour. The client states that when she viewed the property she was told that she could park her car on a small piece of the neighbouring land. The neighbour's land is approximately one acre in size and they have a separate driveway. The client also has her own driveway. She is also unable to receive a clear television signal as the neighbour is building a large extension which is interfering with her TV signal. The client wants to claim an easement of these rights.

Which of the following best represents the client's legal position?

A. The client would be able to make a claim for an easement of parking as the neighbouring land is big enough to accommodate this and it is not infringing too onerously on their own use of the land. The client cannot claim an easement for the right to a television signal as that is too vague.

B. The client would not be able to claim an easement for parking as she has her own driveway, but she will be able to make a claim an easement for the right to the television signal.

C. The client would be able to make a claim for an easement of parking and for the television signal, but only if the same has been in constant use for more than 20 years.

D. The client would not be able to claim an easement for parking as she has her own driveway and she cannot claim an easement for the right to a television signal as that is too vague.

E. The client would be able to make a claim for an easement of parking as the court would consider why the easement is necessary. If the neighbouring land is big enough to accommodate the easement and there is no possibility to park her car on her own driveway then this may be accepted. The client cannot claim an easement for the right to a television signal as that is too vague.

■ ANSWERS TO QUESTIONS

Answers to 'What do you know already?' questions at the start of the chapter

1) The correct answer was C. This is a negative easement and the courts will not recognise any new negative easements because of the restrictive impact if would have on the neighbouring land. All the other answers show examples of positive easements, where there must be some action taken to exercise the right, such as actually walking or driving over the other land.

2) False: this deals with the requirements for an easement. The creation of the easement (whether equitable or otherwise) is not considered until all the *Re Ellenborough* criteria have been satisfied and you can determine that there is an easement.

3) The correct answer was B. The land must be completely unusable, or landlocked, to satisfy the necessity requirements. A shows an easement by common intention, C shows an easement by prescription, D is part of the requirements from *Wheeldon v Burrows* and E would only be correct if the easement had been used for more than 40 years.

4) The correct answer was C – a deed. Remember an express grant is one that is expressly agreed between the parties and there is evidence of that and clear words used. A is incorrect as, again, a verbal

agreement would only satisfy use of the easement for more than 40 years. B is incorrect as this agreement needs to satisfy the strict requirements of being a deed – an agreement written on a piece of paper that does not meet the requirements of a deed would be insufficient. D is incorrect as that shows an easement by prescription and E is incorrect as that is an implied grant by common intention.

5) False. *Wheeldon v Burrows* deals with the creation of easements by implied grant. Prescription will always relate to the long use of an easement, with the minimum term being 20 years.

Answers to end-of-chapter SQE1-style questions

Question 1:

The correct answer was D. This is because necessity requires the land to be completely landlocked. Whilst it may be desirable for her to cross the land, it is not necessary. However, as she has used the right for over 20 years she could make a claim under prescription for long use. Options A and E are incorrect as they are referring to necessity and the land is not completely landlocked. Option B is incorrect as this is looking at an easement under the rule in *Wheeldon v Burrows* and not necessity. Option C is incorrect as it is clearly not the intention of the parties.

Question 2:

The correct answer was E. This is because the client needs continued access to the land, so this will be a reservation of an easement. If possible, it should always be written into a deed to avoid ambiguity in the future, so if the client has this opportunity then that is what he should be advised. Option A is incorrect as necessity requires the land to be completely unusable and landlocked, the question does not give any information on this being a possibility. Option B is incorrect as we do not know that this was the common intention between the parties. Option C is incorrect as he is not granting an easement, he is reserving one for himself and option D is incorrect as you cannot reserve easements, you can only grant them.

Question 3:

The correct answer was B. This is because the easement has been made by a deed and so, providing it is registered, all legal easements will continue to be binding on new owners of the land. Options A and C are incorrect as this is not how a legal easement operates and it may be impossible for the original grantee to enter into a new deed each time the land is sold, especially if they no longer own the adjoining land. Option D is incorrect in this scenario as it is not the best answer available. Whilst there may be a slight possibility that the easement could be implied, we know there is a deed and a legal easement will always trump an equitable one. Option E is incorrect as the owner of dominant land cannot grant themselves an easement – they would reserve themselves an easement.

Question 4:

The correct answer was E. The new owner would still need to use the chimney after the purchase and so this is a derogation from what was expected when the right was granted. A is incorrect as we do not know from the question that the client was using the right before she sold the land. B and C are incorrect as you do not have enough information in the question to determine if either common intention or prescription are a valid option. D is incorrect as the client is not entitled to simply stop access or the use of common services and that would bring about of a claim of an easement in this way.

Question 5:

The correct answer was E. You cannot have an easement to receive radio, telephone or other electronic signals over neighbouring land. The easement is too vague. Just because the client has a drive it does not mean that she has the means to park on it. Parking on the neighbouring drive may be the only possible parking available and so the court would consider all the circumstances. A, B, C and D are all incorrect on either one or both of the necessary elements.

■ KEY CASES, RULES, STATUTES AND INSTRUMENTS

The SQE1 Assessment Specification does not require you to know any case names, or statutory materials for the topic of land law. Despite this, you may find it useful to become familiar with these statues:

Prescription Act 1832

Law of Property Act 1925

Law of Property (Miscellaneous Provisions) Act 1989.

7

Freehold covenants

■ MAKE SURE YOU KNOW

A covenant is a promise between owners of freehold land and this promise regulates the use of that land in a certain way, either requiring one party to do something (positive covenant) or not to do certain things on their own land (restrictive or negative covenant), which must be for the benefit of neighbouring land.

This chapter concerns the enforceability of those freehold covenants either between the original parties to the deed under the privity of contract, or whether the covenants are enforceable between subsequent owners of the land, where you need to demonstrate whether the benefit or the burden of that covenant has passed to a subsequent owner. In the simplest of terms, we are looking at whether the party who currently benefits from a covenant can sue the party who has the burden of that covenant for not complying with it.

This chapter will only consider the rules relating to freehold covenants and they do need to be distinguished from leasehold covenants as there are different rules relating to the ways in which they are enforced. As such, leasehold covenants will be considered separately in **Chapter 5**.

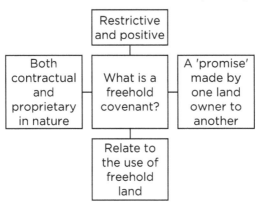

■ SQE ASSESSMENT ADVICE

As you work through this chapter, remember to pay particular attention in your revision to:

- how to identify a covenant
- determining whether the covenant is positive or restrictive in nature
- understanding how to enforce covenants between the original parties
- understanding how to enforce covenants between successors in title
- the importance of building schemes.

■ WHAT DO YOU KNOW ALREADY?

Try answering these questions before reading this chapter. If you find some difficult or can't remember the answers, make a note to look more closely at that subtopic during your revision.

1) What is a covenant?
   a) a promise with future landowners to be liable for breach of any easement
   b) a promise to provide something from the land to neighbouring land
   c) a promise to do something or not to do something on land
   d) a promise with the Local Authority to apply for planning permission for alterations to the property
   e) a promise with the original landowner to pay a yearly sum of money for the breach of any covenants.

   [What are freehold covenants?, page 155]

2) A client owns a large plot of land and builds a house on one half of the land and sells the other half. The deed contains a covenant that the client will plant trees on her retained garden land over the next five years. It also contains a covenant that the owner of the new house cannot keep any pet birds on the property or gardens.

   Which of these covenants is positive and which is restrictive in nature?
   a) They are both restrictive covenants.
   b) They are both positive covenants.
   c) They are neither restrictive nor positive covenants.
   d) Planting trees is restrictive and not keeping birds is positive.
   e) Planting trees is positive and not keeping birds is restrictive.

   [Is the covenant positive or restrictive?, page 156]

3) True or false? Under common law rules the burden of both positive and restrictive covenants can run with the land and bind successors in title.

   [Passing the burden of covenants in law between successors in title, page 158]

4) Which of the following best describes the covenantee?

   a) This is the person who has the benefit of the covenant.

   b) This is the person who has the burden of the covenant.

   c) This only ever relates to the parties named in the original deed.

   d) This is someone who will be awarded damages if there is a breach of covenant.

   e) This is someone who must comply with the restrictive covenants in the deed.

   [Passing of the burden in law and equity, page 157]

5) What does it mean when a covenant must 'touch and concern' the benefited land?

   a) The restrictive covenant must be personal in nature.

   b) The restrictive covenant can benefit land anywhere in the country.

   c) The restrictive covenant must relate to a specific person named in the deeds.

   d) The restrictive covenant must have something to do with the use of the land or the value of the land.

   e) The restrictive covenant only relates to land that is physically adjoining the burdened property.

   [The covenant must touch and concern the land, page 161]

WHAT ARE FREEHOLD COVENANTS?

Freehold covenants are essentially promises between landowners that they will either do something on the land, such as maintain the garden, or that they will not do something, such as not build an extension.

Covenants, unlike easements, are usually quite easy to identify firstly because they must be made in a document and secondly by the wording used. Examples of different freehold covenants will be set out throughout this chapter. Difficulties can arise in trying to identify whether the covenant is still enforceable; this difficulty most commonly arises where there has been a change of ownership of the land.

Freehold covenants are both contractual and proprietary in nature. This is why we need to consider both the legal position and the equitable position when considering the enforceability of covenants.

This chapter will focus on the key elements of freehold covenants and the steps needed to enable you to identify the nature of the covenant and then to determine if it is still enforceable. This should allow you to tackle any SQE questions on this topic.

Is the covenant positive or restrictive?

The first step is to ensure you can identify whether the covenant is **positive** or **restrictive** in nature. This is important so that you can determine if the benefit or the burden has passed to a new landowner and as such whether the covenant is still enforceable.

Key term: positive covenant
A positive covenant is a request to do something on the land, usually involving expenditure of money

Key term: restrictive covenant
A restrictive covenant is a promise to refrain from doing something on the land for the benefit of another person

Positive covenants usually require some expenditure of money; some examples are:
• to construct a habitable dwelling on an area of land within a certain time period
• to paint or re-paint exterior walls or fences every five years.

Restrictive covenants will always require a promise to refrain from doing something on the land; some examples are:
• not to play music between the hours of 11 pm and 7 am.
• not to use any garden land as a driveway.

What is important when determining whether a covenant is positive or restrictive is the substance of the covenant and not necessarily the wording. For example, a covenant stating 'to keep the land as an open space' could possibly be seen as a positive covenant as it is asking the landowner to 'do' something, but it is in fact negative in nature as it is restricting future use of the land in a certain way.

Exam warning

It is important to identify at the outset whether the covenant is positive or negative in nature as it will completely change the result of whether it is enforceable against future owners, ie, whether the benefit and burden of the covenant run with the land. So, do always take the time to consider that initial point.

We will now consider a number of different steps that will determine whether the covenant is in fact enforceable. These are:
- Has the burden of the covenant passed in law?
- Has the benefit of the covenant passed in law?
- Has the burden of the covenant passed in equity?
- Has the benefit of the covenant passed in equity?
- Has the covenant been properly registered?

We will consider these in turn.

PASSING OF THE BURDEN IN LAW AND EQUITY

Firstly, make sure you can identify who is the **covenantor** and who is the **covenantee**.

Key term: covenantor

Covenantor: the person who is bound to carry out the 'promise' of the covenant.

Key term: covenantee

Covenantee: the person who makes and can enforce the covenant.

If you know you are dealing with a question concerning the original covenantor and the original covenantee, then this can be easy to resolve as we will demonstrate next.

Passing the burden in law between the original parties

It is straightforward to determine whether the burden or the benefit of the covenant has passed when you are considering the original parties to the covenant. The diagram shown in **Figure 7.1** will explain this further.

Figure 7.1: How to determine the covenantor and the covenantee

If we assume that Sophie sells to Romesh and the deed specifies that he must not keep any pet birds on the property, this means that Sophie is the *covenantee* as she has the *benefit* of the covenant; she is the one who can enforce the covenant and Romesh is the *covenantor* as he is subject to the *burden* of the covenant or the promise – he is the one who must carry out the promise.

This puts the parties back to basic contract principles; if Romesh does not comply with the covenant then Sophie can look to enforce this breach of the contract by taking court action or obtaining an injunction. Equally, Romesh could sue Sophie if she does not comply with any covenants in her deeds which are there for the benefit of his land. This is the principle of privity of contract and only the parties to a contract can sue or be sued under it.

So, whilst dealing with the burden of any covenants between the original parties to the deed is straightforward, we now need to consider the more complex rules for dealing with the enforceability of covenants between future owners of the land, otherwise known as successors in title.

PASSING THE BURDEN OF COVENANTS IN LAW BETWEEN SUCCESSORS IN TITLE

An initial point which is important to note is that there can be no mixing of these rules. That is, for example, if the burden of a covenant passes in law then it will only be enforceable if the benefit of the covenant has also passed in law; this should become clear as we work through the chapter.

We can keep this section relatively brief: under common law rules any covenant, either positive or negative, cannot run with the land. **Figure 7.2** explains this further.

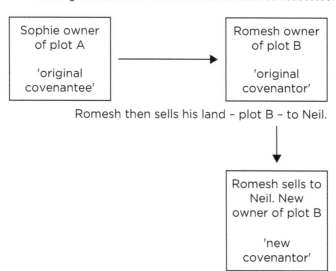

Figure 7.2: Passing of the burden in law between subsequent owners

The original covenant of 'not to keep any pet birds on the property' remains in the deed but, as Neil was not an original party to the deed, Sophie could not sue him using basic contractual principles if Neil subsequently decided to keep pet birds on the land. If Sophie wants to enforce the covenant against Neil she will need to demonstrate that the burden of the covenant has passed to him, in other words, we need to establish whether the burden has 'run' with the land. Sophie remains the original party to the deed and so the benefit of the covenant remains with her.

Exam warning

If you receive a question which refers to land which is subject to a covenant being sold in this way, then it may help to draw a small plan to map out the plots of land as shown in **Figure 7.2.** This should hopefully make it clear as to whether you are considering the passing of the benefit or the burden of the covenant.

As such, using our example in **Figure 7.2**, Neil would not be subject to any covenants in common law, so we would need to consider if it has run in equity, which we will look at later in this chapter.

There is one exception to this rule that you may need to know for this SQE1 exam:

- The doctrine of mutual burden and benefit:
  - If a landowner enjoys certain benefits on the land, but with those benefits come certain burdens then he may only receive the benefits if he also takes on the burden. An example of this would be if someone had the benefit of using common corridors in a shared building but they were not prepared to keep their portion of those corridors in good use or keep them clean.

Questions on easements are likely to look at the more complex arrangements on covenants, so when dealing with this type of question you will need to consider the equitable rules which do allow the passing of a restrictive covenant to successors in title in certain circumstances. This is also why it is important to initially determine whether the covenant is positive or restrictive in nature at the outset as different rules do apply to the different covenants.

Figure 7.3 will give you a visual reminder of these initial steps.

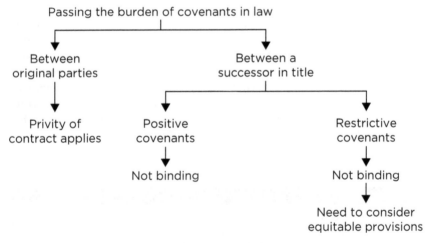

Figure 7.3: Passing the burden of covenants in law

PASSING THE BENEFIT OF COVENANTS IN LAW BETWEEN SUCCESSORS IN TITLE

We have looked at the passing of the burden at common law so we now need to consider whether the *benefit* of either a positive or restrictive covenant has passed in law. A quick reminder, this would arise where the original covenantee sells or transfers their land which has the benefit of the original covenant. This can be done in the following ways:

- by express assignment under s 36 LPA 1925. This requires the original covenantee to assign the benefit of the covenant at the same time as the transfer of the land to the successor in title
- by the Contracts (Rights of Third Parties) Act 1999. If the third party is identified by name they will enjoy the same benefit
- by s 56 LPA 1925. If the third party was identified at the time the covenant was made then that person may benefit from the covenant.

For the benefit of the covenant to run in law several conditions must be met:

- the covenant must 'touch and concern' the land
- the original covenantee must have held legal estate in the benefited land
- the successor in title must obtain their title from or under the original covenantee, and
- the benefit of the covenant must have been intended to run with the land. This can be proven in one of three ways:
  - by express annexation
  - by implied annexation
  - by s 78 LPA 1925.

We shall briefly look through these four conditions as follows:

The covenant must 'touch and concern' the land

The benefit of a covenant will pass to a successor in title, provided the covenant is beneficial to the land itself and not simply a benefit to the original covenantee personally. A good tip is to look at whether the covenant affects the way in which the land can be used or its value.

Revision tip

Being personal in nature refers to it being a promise made to a specific person, so, using the example demonstrated in **Figure 7.2**, Sophie's covenant may have failed this criterion if the covenant had specifically stated it was for the benefit of a specific third party who, for example, lived at number 10.

At the date of the covenant, the original covenantee held a legal estate in the benefited land

So, the covenantee must hold one of the recognised legal estates in land. This was considered in **Chapter 1**; those are freehold and leasehold. The benefit of a covenant would not pass if the original covenantee only held an equitable interest in the land.

The successor in title must obtain their title from or under the original covenantee

Pre-1925 covenants required that the successor in title held the same legal estate as the original covenantee, so if the original legal estate was freehold then the successor in title must also hold a freehold estate in the land. However, post-1925 covenants do not have the same requirement, so where the original covenantee held a freehold estate but then later grants a leasehold estate, the covenant can still be enforced by that successor in title.

The benefit of the covenant was intended to run with the land

This is where you may hear the term 'annexed' or '**annexation**', which can be separated into the three categories set out below:
• by express annexation
• by implied annexation
• by s 78 LPA 1925.

> **Key term: annexation**
>
> The benefit of a covenant will be permanently fixed to the land and so will pass automatically upon a future conveyance or transfer of that land.

• by express annexation

This is where some form of words of annexation are used in the deed, expressly stating that the covenant will benefit a specific piece of land, and that it is intended to pass to successive owners of the land. In these circumstances, the benefit of the covenant will pass automatically with the land to future owners.

• by implied annexation

The Court may be prepared to imply that the benefit of the covenant will pass to successors in title if the facts of the case show the identity of the land being benefited is sufficiently clear. However, these are used very rarely due to the availability of both express annexation and statutory provisions of s 78 LPA 25.

- Statutory Annexation under Section 78 LPA 1925

This is the most likely method of annexation to apply in a problem question. It means that every covenant which is held to touch and concern the land will automatically be annexed to the land in question, with the benefit of that covenant automatically passing to successors in title in equity. This has in some way resolved the issues of express and implied annexation.

Practice example 7.1 explains these four conditions in more detail.

Practice example 7.1

Dean owns two adjoining properties, numbers 2 and 4 Beswick Close. Dean sells number 4 to Kenny so Dean is the original covenantee under the conveyance and Kenny is the original covenantor. Within the conveyance there is a covenant stating, 'with and for the benefit of Dean and his successors in title and the owners of number 2 Beswick Close, not to use number 4 Beswick Close for occupation by more than one family at a time'.

Dean sells his property to Marie. Kenny then starts construction work to convert number 4 Beswick Close into a house of multiple occupation to let out to students. Can Marie enforce this covenant against Kenny?

Yes, she can.
- **Firstly, she can prove that the covenant 'touches and concerns' the land as covenants of this type have been held to satisfy this condition.**
- **Dean held legal title at the time the covenant was made and so the second condition is met.**
- **Marie's title can easily be traced back to the original conveyance made between Dean and Kenny.**
- **Finally, it is also intended, by the wording of the deed, that the benefit of this covenant would pass to successors in title.**

Figure 7.4 will give you a visual reminder of these initial steps.

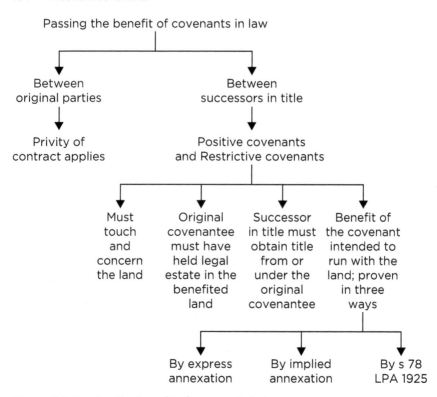

Figure 7.4: Passing the benefit of covenants in law

Having considered the rules for the passing of the burden and benefit in law, we now need to consider the passing of the burden and the benefit of a covenant in equity.

PASSING THE BURDEN OF COVENANTS IN EQUITY BETWEEN SUCCESSORS IN TITLE

Equity only permits the burden of *restrictive* covenants to be passed. So, if the question talks about the burden of a positive covenant being passed in equity you can be sure that is incorrect. It is only the benefit of a restrictive covenant that can pass in equity, which we will consider later in this chapter.

Four conditions must be fulfilled for the burden of a restrictive covenant to pass to a successor in title, or 'run with the land'. Those are:

• The covenant must be negative (or restrictive) in nature.
• At the date of the covenant, the covenantee retained land which was benefited by the covenant.

- The covenant must 'touch and concern' the land.
- The burden of the covenant must be intended to run with the land.

Practice example 7.2 explains these further.

Practice example 7.2

James sold an area of open land in the centre of a busy city to Marian; this sale was by way of a conveyance which stated that the open space must be kept 'uncovered with any buildings in neat ornamental order', which was to ensure the land was preserved for leisure activities. Marian later sells this land on to Michael who is aware of the covenant at the time he purchased but refuses to acknowledge it and proceeds to make plans to build on the land. James then brings legal proceedings against Michael and seeks an injunction to prevent the anticipated breach.

Can James seek an injunction on the basis that Michael, as successor in title to Marian, was bound to comply with the restrictive covenant?

These are the facts of *Tulk v Moxhay* [1848]. The court held that Michael was bound by the restrictive covenant in equity. This was on the basis that it was intended that the covenant would run with the land and Michael, as successor in title, had been given notice of its existence. Michael was therefore bound by the equitable restrictive covenant not to build on the land. This case also laid out the four conditions that must be met for the burden of an equitable restrictive covenant to pass to a successor in title, which are set out above.

We shall now look through those conditions as follows:

- the covenant must be negative in nature

As we already know, a negative covenant is one which restricts a party from doing something with the land. The burden of positive covenants will not pass in equity.

- at the date of the covenant, the covenantee retained land which was benefited by the covenant

If someone owns a large area of land, but then sells all of this off and no longer owns any land which benefits from the covenants, they will be unable to enforce the same in equity. Consider **Practice example 7.3** to see this in practice.

Practice example 7.3

Mr Allen purchased a large piece of land from the Local Authority with a covenant that he would not build on a small piece of the land. Mr Allen then sold the land to his wife who began construction on all of the land, including the small part subject to the covenant. Can the Local Authority enforce the restrictive covenant against Mrs Allen?

These are the facts of *London CC v Allen* [1914]. The Council were unsuccessful in enforcing this covenant as they did not own any land which benefited from the covenant at the time the covenant was granted. This may be one of the reasons for the development of building schemes, which we will consider later in the chapter.

• the covenant must 'touch and concern' the land

A covenant will 'touch and concern' if it has something to do with the use of the land or the value of the land and the covenant is not personal in nature. There would, for example, be no use in a restrictive covenant stating that there should be no noise between 11 pm and 6 am if the land with the benefit of that covenant was located 100 miles from the burdened land. No one on the benefited land would ever hear the noise.

• the burden of the covenant must be intended to run with the covenantee's land

In practical questions you may see this worded as 'I Winston Clark covenant on behalf of myself and my heirs and assigns', which demonstrates that the original covenantee intended the burden to run with the land. This wording is somewhat now redundant and after 1925 it was assumed that covenants relating to land will always run with the land unless it is specified to the contrary in the deed.

So, for this part, unless you receive a question which specifically states the deed was made before 1925, or there are any exceptions in the deed, you can assume that this condition is satisfied.

Figure 7.5 will give you a visual reminder of these initial steps.

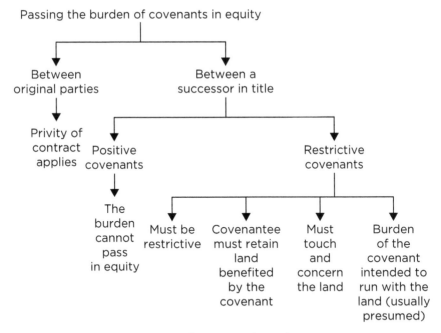

Figure 7.5: Passing the burden of covenants in equity

The final point to consider is the equitable rules relating to the passing of the benefit of a covenant in equity.

PASSING THE BENEFIT OF COVENANTS IN EQUITY BETWEEN SUCCESSORS IN TITLE

Again, that quick reminder that, for the burden of the covenant to pass in equity, the benefit of the covenant must be shown to pass in equity as well. The benefit of both positive and restrictive covenants can pass in equity, but several conditions need to be met:

• the covenant must 'touch and concern' the land
• the successor in title to the original covenantee must hold a legal or equitable estate in the land
• the benefit of the covenant was intended to run with the land. This can be separated into a further three categories:
    – by express, implied or statutory annexation under s 78 LPA 1925
    – by express or implied assignment
    – the land in question is part of a 'building scheme'.

The first two conditions have been dealt with earlier in the chapter, so we will now consider how the benefit of the covenant can run with the land.

By express, implied or s 78 LPA 1925 annexation

This was considered in detail within the 'passing of the benefit of covenants in law', but a brief recap of those general rules is set out below:

- by express annexation

Where some form of words of annexation are used in the deed, expressly stating that the covenant will benefit a specific piece of land, and that it is intended to pass to successive owners of the land. In these circumstances, the benefit of the covenant will pass automatically with the land to future owners.

- by implied annexation

The court may be prepared to imply that the benefit of the covenant will pass to successors in title if the facts of the case show the identity of the land being benefited is sufficiently clear. However, these are used very rarely due to the availability of both express annexation and statutory provisions of s 78 LPA 25.

- Statutory Annexation under Section 78 LPA 1925

This is the most likely method of annexation to apply in a problem question. It means that every covenant which is held to touch and concern the land will automatically be annexed to the land in question, with the benefit of that covenant automatically passing to successors in title in equity. This has in some way resolved the issues of express and implied annexation.

Express or implied assignment

An **assignment** is where the land is transferred, and it is important to be mindful of the differences between assignment and **annexation**.

Key term: annexation

Annexation happens once the covenant is entered into and it attaches the benefit of the covenant to the land.

Key term: assignment

Assignment is when the land is transferred, which could be many years after annexation has taken place. The benefit of the covenant can be lost if a chain of indemnity is broken, ie, is not *assigned* in the deed to a successor in title.

This type of assignment transfers the benefit of that covenant to a certain person. This mode of transmission means the benefit will only run with the land if words of assignment are contained in the subsequent deeds.

Revision tip

Implied assignment may be seen to hold little significance since the introduction of s 78 LPA 1925, but express assignment is still of great importance when dealing with covenants.

Assignment is set out in three broad criteria:
- The land must be capable of benefiting from the covenant.
- It must be possible to identify the land.
- The assignment of the covenant must take place at the same time as the transfer between owners.

This can be shown in **Practice example 7.4**.

Practice example 7.4

Demi owns a large plot of land and builds a house known as 'The Poppy'. She sells a parcel of land to Nicola and the deed contains a restrictive covenant not to run any business from the land. The covenant is not annexed to the land as the deed states that the benefit of this covenant will not pass without express assignment. Demi then sells 'The Poppy' to Harvey and in doing so assigns, in the deed, the benefit of the covenant to him. If Nicola then starts to run any business on her land Harvey could enforce that covenant.

Harvey then later transfers 'The Poppy' to Leyton but he forgets to assign the benefit of the covenant in the deed. Can Leyton enforce any breach of this covenant against Nicola?

No, whilst the land is capable of benefiting from the covenant and it is possible to identify the land, here the 'chain of assignment' (also known as the chain of indemnity) has been broken so Leyton cannot enforce the covenant and Harvey is unable to rectify this at a later date as he is no longer the owner and is unable to assign the benefit. S.78 will not operate to save this covenant as the deed makes it very clear that the covenant will not pass without express assignment; that would be contrary intention to s 78 and it would not override that written condition.

Revision tip

This is a scenario that you may need to consider in a SQE1 exam question and so consideration of assignment is important as a homeowner claiming they have the benefit of a covenant must show that the transfer document or deed contained an effective assignment.

The land in question is part of a 'building scheme'

This relates to a defined piece of land which is then sold off into plots to different purchasers. These are commonly associated with new build housing estates where large numbers of houses are built and then subsequently sold and occupied by different homeowners, leaving the original owner, the covenantee, with no land in their ownership.

This means the enforceability of covenants explored in this chapter could not apply as the builder does not retain any land in their ownership. This would leave the homeowners with no way of enforcing these covenants or benefiting from them. The idea behind a building scheme is that the covenants are enforceable between the present homeowners and the covenants continue to benefit each house on that housing estate.

There are two main prerequisites to establishing whether a building scheme exists:
• evidence of a common intention between all purchasers that the area of land is to be sold in plots and
• a clear intention that all purchasers of the individual plots will be subject to those mutual and reciprocal covenants.

Consider **Practice example 7.5** to explore this further.

Practice example 7.5

Allan owned a large plot of land known as the Seaham View Estate. He died and the estate was sold off in plots. There were nine transfers in total, the first four were administered by Allan's daughter and the other five by his brother. They had identical restrictive covenants within them detailing what could be built upon these plots of land. One of the purchasers planned to build on the plot in a way that would have been inconsistent with the terms of this covenant. Could this purchaser claim that they were not bound by the covenants and no building scheme was established as there was no common vendor in line with the authority at the time?

This is based on the facts of *Re Dolphin's Conveyance* (1970) in which the High Court held that a building scheme had been established despite there being no common vendor. Considering all the other circumstances of the case there was a very clear intention that the covenants were to be enforceable by each owner against all other owners. The covenants were clearly for the mutual benefit of every homeowner on the estate.

An important note that these building schemes do apply to the passing of the benefit only, the burden of the covenant still needs to be identified in the way considered earlier in this chapter.

You may wish to follow **Figure 7.6** if you need to remind yourself of the principles to be considered here.

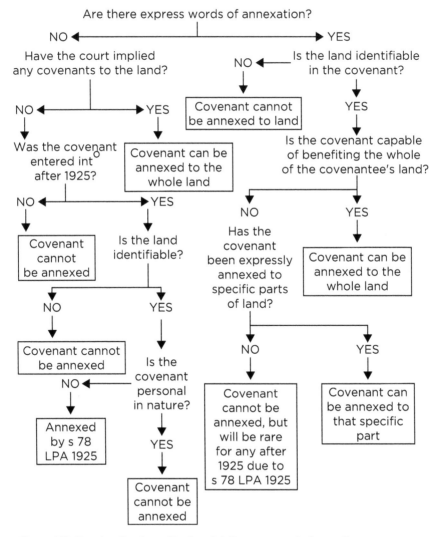

Figure 7.6: Passing the benefit of restrictive covenants in equity

PASSING THE BENEFIT AND BURDEN OF COVENANTS IN LAW AND EQUITY

It may be helpful to recap these principles covered so far and returning to the original scenario shown in **Figure 7.1** and **Figure 7.2**, but we have also now included a further sale between the original owner of plot A, Sophie, who has now sold her land to Lucas. The diagram in **Figure 7.7** will explain this further.

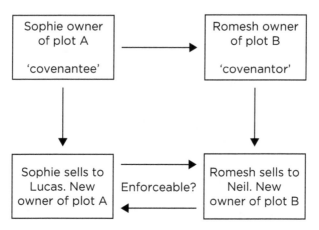

Figure 7.7: How to determine which route to use

The parties to the covenant are shown below.

We can now consider the ways in which Neil and Lucas, the new owners, can enforce the benefit or the burden of the restrictive covenants between them, which is explained further in **Figure 7.8**.

PROTECTION OF FREEHOLD COVENANTS

The importance of registration of covenants has been discussed in **Chapter 3** and **Chapter 4**, but it is important to recap these principles here and the different rules that apply to registered or unregistered land.

Registered land

S 29 Land Registration Act 2002 will apply and states that in registered land, the burden of a covenant in equity can pass, provided that:

a) the successor in title is a purchaser for valuable consideration, so they are paying the market value for the property.

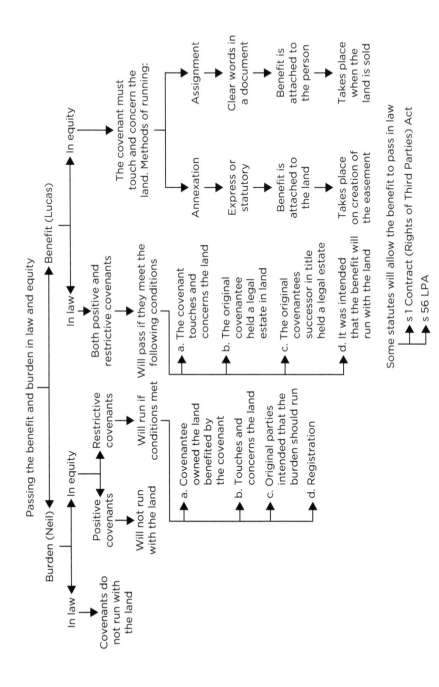

Figure 7.8: Passing the benefit and burden of covenants in law and equity

b) a notice has been registered against the title of the burdened land. This will then appear in the charges register of the title deeds.

You may wish to refer to **Chapter 3** for information on the registration of covenants in the title register.

Unregistered land

For covenants created before 1st January 1926 the doctrine of notice rule applies and so easements do not need to be registered to take effect, which means if you are a purchaser for valuable consideration and you have not been notified of the covenant, then you will not be subject to the covenant.

For covenants created after 1st January 1926 (the implementation of the LPA 1925), these must be registered as a Class D(ii) land charge against the name of the original covenantor and would be registered as a notice against the burdened title upon first registration.

You may wish to follow **Figure 7.9** if you need to remind yourself of the principles to be considered here.

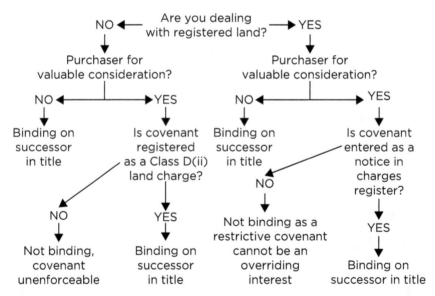

Figure 7.9: Passing the burden of a restrictive covenant by registration

■ KEY POINT CHECKLIST

This chapter has covered the following key knowledge points. You can use these to structure your revision around, making sure to recall the key details for each point, as covered in this chapter.

• The starting point is to determine whether the covenant is positive or restrictive in nature. You then need to consider who the covenantor and the covenantee are as the ability to enforce a covenant will depend entirely on these initial points.

• Enforceability will also depend on whether ownership of the land is still with the original covenantee or covenantor, or whether ownership has changed.

• Once you have determined these initial points you must then consider whether it is the benefit or the burden of the covenant as, again, different rules apply to the running of the covenant and whether it will be enforceable. Remember, the burden of a covenant is usually demonstrated by someone being prevented from doing something on their own land, such as using their garden as a drive. The benefit of a covenant is usually demonstrated by someone showing they would be disadvantaged if the covenant was breached, such as a neighbour in a block of flats playing loud music between the hours of 11 pm and 6 am.

• In common law, the burden of both positive and negative covenants cannot run with the land. In equity, positive covenants do not run with the land but several conditions must be met for the burden of negative covenants to run, which are: the covenant must be negative in nature, at the date of the covenant there must be land that can benefit from the covenant, the covenant must 'touch and concern' the land and the burden of the covenant must be intended to run with the land.

• In common law, for the benefit of a covenant to run with the land several conditions must be met which are: the covenant must touch and concern the land, the original covenantee must have held the legal estate when the covenant was made, the successor in title must have obtained their legal estate from the original covenantee and the benefit of the covenant was intended to run with the land.

• In common law some statutes also allow the benefit of a covenant to pass, such as s 1 Contracts (Rights of third parties) Act 1999 and s 56 Law of Property Act 1925.

• In equity, for the benefit of a covenant to run with the land several conditions must be met, which are: the covenant must touch and concern the land, the original covenantee must have held the legal or equitable estate when the covenant was made, the successor in title must have a legal or equitable estate in the land and the benefit of the covenant must have been intended to run with the land.

- You may need to consider annexation or assignment of the benefit of a covenant in equity. Annexation can be express, implied or statutory annexation under s 78 LPA 1925. Assignment can be express or implied.
- The covenant may also form part of a building scheme and so will be mutually enforceable between the current owners. The key to identifying these is whether the land was common ownership of one person and they have then sold individual plots of that land to others. If they retain no land for themselves then it may be part of a building scheme.
- For a covenant to be enforceable you will also need to consider whether the land is registered or unregistered and whether the covenant has been properly registered either as a notice on the charges register (registered land) or as a D(ii) Land Charge (unregistered). If registered as a land charge it is enforceable whether the new owner has checked the register or not.

■ KEY TERMS AND CONCEPTS

- positive covenant (**page 156**)
- negative covenant (**page 156**)
- covenantor (**page 157**)
- covenantee (**page 157**)
- annexation (**page 162**)
- assignment (**page 168**)

■ SQE1-STYLE QUESTIONS

QUESTION 1

A client has sought legal advice as his neighbour's roof has recently fallen into disrepair and he wants to see if he can do anything about it. He shows his solicitor a deed in which the neighbour gave a covenant for the benefit of the client's house to: 'not to let the roof fall into disrepair'.

Which of the following best describes why the client is likely to be able to sue the neighbour under this covenant?

A. The building scheme exception will apply.
B. The doctrine of mutual benefit and burden will apply.

C. It is a positive covenant.

D. It is a restrictive covenant.

E. The neighbour was the original party to the deed.

QUESTION 2

A client has recently purchased a house and there is a covenant in the deeds stating: 'the purchaser and his successors in title must paint the fences every five years in white paint'. The previous owner owned the house for ten years and the fence was never painted.

Which of the following best describes what action the client must now take?

A. No action is required as this is a positive covenant and is not binding on a successor in title.

B. No action is required as this is a negative covenant and is not binding on a successor in title.

C. The client must paint the fence immediately or risk being in breach of the positive covenant.

D. The client must paint the fence immediately or risk being in breach of the restrictive covenant.

E. The covenant has already been breached and so the client will now receive a fine.

QUESTION 3

A client has asked for some legal advice. When he was considering selling his house two years ago he knew that his neighbour would be really upset if someone moved in with cats as they would ruin her vegetable patch. He included a restrictive covenant in the deed to say the purchaser cannot keep cats on the property. He sells the house and the new owner complies with the covenant. A year later, the new owner sells the property again and this subsequent owner has moved in with three cats. The neighbour calls the client very upset by this as he promised her this would never happen.

Which of the following best describes whether the client is able to enforce this covenant against the current owner?

A. The client can enforce the covenant against the current owner as she is bound by the terms of the deed.

B. The client can enforce the covenant against the current owner as it is a negative covenant and they are always enforceable.

C. The client can enforce the covenant against the current owner as it is a positive covenant and they are always enforceable.

D. The client cannot enforce the covenant against the current owner as it is a negative covenant and they are never enforceable.

E. The client cannot enforce the covenant against the current owner as he no longer owns any land to be benefited by the covenant.

QUESTION 4

A building company have built ten houses on separate plots of land, which they then sell off individually to new owners. Each house is subject to the same covenants in their deeds, including a covenant stating that the owners cannot park any caravans on the driveway. A client purchased her house directly from the building company five years ago; her neighbours also bought directly from the building company but have recently sold their house to someone new who has moved in and parked his caravan on his driveway. This is blocking the client's view over the open fields.

What best describes the legal position of the client?

A. The client would need to write to her Local Authority to complain.

B. The client can only ask the new neighbour if he would be willing to move his caravan so her view is no longer blocked.

C. The client can take legal action to enforce these covenants as they are considered a building scheme and directly enforceable between property owners.

D. The client would need to contact the original building company to take legal action against the new neighbour.

E. The client can only take action for her breach of her right to light and would need to file a claim with the court.

QUESTION 5

A client has recently purchased some freehold land which contains a covenant with the local drainage authority specifying that the drainage authority would maintain the riverbanks to prevent flooding of the land. The client granted a lease over the land to a third party who wishes to use the land as a farm. This means that the client owns the freehold estate and the third party holds the leasehold estate in the land. The land has recently flooded, meaning there has been a breach of the covenant by the local drainage authority.

Which of the following best represents the party who can enforce this covenant against the drainage authority?

A. Only the client can enforce the covenant as he holds the freehold estate in land and enforcement of covenants can only be between the freehold estate owners.

B. Only the third party can enforce the covenant as he holds the leasehold estate in land and enforcement of covenant can only be made by the most recent estate owner.

C. Neither the client or the third party can enforce the covenant and it can only be enforced by the original covenantee.

D. Both the client and the third party can enforce the covenant as the benefit of the covenant has passed to them by common law.

E. Both the client and the third party can enforce the covenant as the benefit of the covenant has passed to them by equity.

■ ANSWERS TO QUESTIONS

Answers to 'What do you know already?' questions at the start of the chapter

1) The correct answer was C. Covenants are essentially promises between landowners to do something on the land (positive covenant) or to not do something (negative covenant). A is incorrect as whilst they may seem similar in nature, easements and covenants are separate proprietary rights. B is incorrect as this is more fitting of a profit, which is again similar to an easement. D is incorrect as planning permission has nothing to do with covenants in this sense. It is possible to have a covenant which requires planning permission to be sought for alterations, but the covenant is not made with the Local Authority. E is incorrect as penalty payments are a remedy for a breach of covenant.

2) The correct answer was E. Planting trees is a clear example of a positive covenant, it requires the landowner to take some positive action or spend money to comply with the covenant. Not keeping birds is a clear example of a restrictive covenant; it prevents the landowner from doing something on their own land. This is why all of the other answers can be discounted.

3) The correct answer was false. This is the opposite of passing the burden of both positive and restrictive covenants under common law rules. They cannot run with the land and cannot bind successors

in title. You need to consider the equitable rules to determine if the burden runs with the land.

4) The correct answer was A. The covenantee is always the person who either makes the original covenant, or who can enforce the covenant if it has passed to a successor in title. B and E are incorrect as they describe the covenantor. C is incorrect as, if the covenant has passed to a successor in title, then they would also be referred to as the covenantee. D is incorrect as, although damages may be awarded for a breach of covenant, that is never a guarantee.

5) The correct answer was D. To 'touch and concern' the land must mean that it has something to do with that land and it will be of a benefit to that land, so the land which benefits from the covenant cannot be too far away and shows it must improve the land in some way.

Answers to end-of-chapter SQE1-style questions

Question 1:
The correct answer was E. This is because the neighbour is the original party to the deed and still the legal owner of the property, so it will always be enforceable against him. It is only if he then sells the property that you may need to consider whether it could be a building scheme, which is why option A is incorrect. Option B would not be the best answer as you do not have enough information to determine if this would apply. Options C and D are incorrect as it does not matter whether the covenant is positive or restrictive, what is required is proof that it is enforceable.

Question 2:
The correct answer was A. This is because this is a positive covenant, one requiring him to do something, usually at his own expense (buying paint) and so would not be enforceable on him as a future owner. Option B is incorrect as negative covenants are binding. Options C, D and E are incorrect as he is not bound by the covenant; they do not pass to a successor in title unless they have expressly agreed to the same.

Question 3:
The correct answer was E. This is because he cannot enforce a covenant where he does not own any land which benefited from the covenant at the time it was granted, which is why option A is incorrect. C is incorrect as this is not a positive covenant. B and D are incorrect as negative covenants are enforceable, but not by people who no longer have a connection to the land which benefits from the covenant.

Question 4:

The correct answer was C. This is because the client may wish to ask the neighbour to move his caravan; if he does not do so she would be able to enforce the covenant as it could be considered part of a building scheme. The original builder no longer owns any of the land and the building scheme is a way of allowing the landowners to enforce the covenants between themselves, which is why option D is incorrect. A is incorrect as the local authority would not have any involvement in the enforcement of private covenants. B is a possible option and would seem the most civil approach, but it is not a legal remedy for the client. E is incorrect as the client may not have a right to light and this could be a futile court application.

Question 5:

The correct answer was D. This is because to enforce a covenant at common law you must own the legal estate; it does not specify whether this must be freehold or leasehold, which is why option A is incorrect. The only requirement of ownership of a legal estate is that it must be any legal estate. Covenants can be enforced by both the freehold and the leasehold owners. B is incorrect as the client is the original party to the deed and so is still able to take enforcement action by way of privity of contract. Option C is incorrect as covenants can be transferred to successors in title, they do not stop with the original parties to the deed. E is incorrect as the covenant has passed by common law and not equity.

■ KEY CASES, RULES, STATUTES AND INSTRUMENTS

The SQE1 Assessment Specification does not require you to know any case names, or statutory materials for the topic of land law. Despite this, you may find it useful to become familiar with these statutes:

Law of Property Act 1925

Land Registration Act 2002.

8

Mortgages

■ MAKE SURE YOU KNOW

This chapter will focus on the key elements of mortgages, looking at enforceability of mortgage terms, priority of mortgages, the mortgagee's powers and duties and protection of mortgagors and other third parties with an interest in the land. This will enable you to tackle any SQE1 questions on this topic.

■ SQE ASSESSMENT ADVICE

As you work through this chapter, remember to pay particular attention in your revision to:

- how the mortgage was created
- the rights and remedies of the mortgagor
- the rights and remedies of the mortgagee
- the priority of mortgages.

■ WHAT DO YOU KNOW ALREADY?

Try answering these questions before reading this chapter. If you find some difficult or can't remember the answers, make a note to look more closely at that subtopic during your revision.

1) What is a legal mortgage?
   a) a legal agreement relating to the exchange of title deeds between the two parties
   b) a legal agreement relating to a loan of money in exchange for legal interests over land or property
   c) a legal agreement or promise to refrain from or not do something on land
   d) a legal agreement with the Local Authority to provide planning permission for alterations to the property at some point in the future
   e) a promise with the original landowner to pay a yearly sum of money for the property for life.
   [Legal mortgages, page 185]

2) True or false? The party who grants a mortgage is the homeowner.
   [What is a mortgage?, page 184]

3) What remedies are available to a mortgagee if there is a breach of any terms of the mortgage conditions?
   a) they have an equitable right to redeem
   b) they have protection from any 'clogs and fetters' in the conditions
   c) amongst other remedies, they have the right to payment
   d) protection from undue influence
   e) general protection under consumer rights legislation.
   [Enforceability of mortgage terms, page 187]

4) Which best describes the position of a cohabitee who wishes to try and postpone any possession proceedings brought by a mortgagee?
   a) They have no right to be party to the proceedings as they hold no legal interest in the mortgaged property.

b) If they can demonstrate that they are a connected person they will automatically be successful in having the proceedings postponed.

c) If they can demonstrate that they are a connected person and can prove they have the ability to meet the debts then they will automatically be successful in having the proceedings postponed.

d) If they can demonstrate that they are a connected person and can prove they have the ability to meet the debts, then they can apply to be joined to the proceedings and ask the court to consider their position to postpone proceedings.

e) If they can demonstrate that they are a connected person they will be joined to the proceedings but would have to pay the mortgage in full to have the proceedings postponed.

[The right to payment, page 195]

5) When would a power of sale by a mortgagee arise?

a) where the mortgage is made by a deed

b) where notice of any default has been served to the mortgagor and three months have elapsed without full payment of the debt

c) where some interest under the mortgage is in arrears and unpaid for two months after becoming due

d) where there has been a breach of any other term of the mortgage

e) where the mortgage is made by a deed, the legal date of redemption has passed and there is no clause expressly excluding the power of sale.

[Power of sale, page 197]

WHAT IS A MORTGAGE?

A general definition of a mortgage is that it is a legal agreement relating to a loan of money in exchange for legal interest over land or property. This legal agreement is then discharged upon the full repayment of the loan by the **mortgagor** to the **mortgagee**.

There is always confusion over these terms and there is a common misconception that the company or person providing the money is the one who *grants* the mortgage, but they do not. The lender cannot grant something over land which they do not own. Consider this to a similar position as a homeowner granting someone a right of way over their land: they own the land and so they grant the right – the third party could not grant themselves this right of way. Similarly with mortgages, the homeowner owns the land and so they *grant* the mortgage to a lender in exchange for the financial contribution from that lender.

Key term: mortgagor

The mortgagor is the borrower, so the person who borrows the money, for that loan of money, will grant a mortgage to the lender.

Key term: mortgagee

A mortgagee is the lender, so a person or financial institution who lends the money to the homeowner, and in return they obtain a proprietary interest in that person's land or property.

HOW ARE MORTGAGES CREATED?

The first step when dealing with a SQE exam question relating to mortgages is to consider how it has been created. This is split into two general provisions:

- legal mortgages and
- equitable mortgages

We shall look at these in turn to ensure you can understand how a mortgage may be created.

Legal mortgages

A legal mortgage is a mortgage which is created in accordance with certain formalities which comply with s 1 and s 2 Law of Property (Miscellaneous Provisions) Act 1989. It must also be registered on the mortgagor's title deeds, as set out in **Chapter 4**. This means that the mortgagee will hold a legal interest in the mortgagor's land until the loan is repaid in full. The mortgagor would not be able to sell or otherwise dispose of the land unless the mortgage is repaid in full. **Practice example 8.1** explains this further.

Practice example 8.1

David wants to buy a property for £125,000 and will be borrowing (or granting a mortgage to the lender) an amount of £106,000 from the Tyne and Wear Building Society. He only wants to keep the mortgage for ten years. How would a valid legal mortgage be created in this scenario?

> Both David and the Tyne and Wear Building Society would need to enter into a legally binding contract. This is demonstrated by David signing a mortgage deed that complies with s 1 LP(MP)A 1989 which must then be registered with HM Land Registry. His mortgage agreement with the Tyne and Wear Building Society would stipulate the terms of the mortgage as agreed between them both.
>
> If David then wanted to sell the property before the end of the agreed ten-year term he can do so providing he repays all of the remaining loan amount in full, which is usually achieved by using the proceeds of sale. This would then cancel the contract and the mortgage can be removed from the title deeds.

Legal mortgages are the most common way of creating mortgages and we shall consider some of the points raised in the above example as we work through this chapter. There is of course the possibility to create a legal mortgage in unregistered land, and that has been considered within **Chapter 3**. We will now consider how to create equitable mortgages.

Equitable mortgages

An equitable mortgage is one which does not grant the mortgagee a legal interest in the mortgagor's land. These generally arise in two situations.

• where the mortgagor only holds an **equitable interest** in the land

This would not require a formal deed, but an assignment of the equitable interest to the mortgagee. This may arise in, for example, the case where someone has a life interest in land under a trust deed and so they do not own the legal estate in land.

• where there is a defective legal mortgage

This can arise in a number of situations, but usually where there has been forgery on the part of one of the mortgagors, or where there has been an attempt to grant a formal legal mortgage, but it has failed for either a defective deed or failure to register with HM Land Registry.

Key term: equitable interest

Equitable interest is a form of ownership or legal interest in land that stems from certain actions, or inactions of a party, or as a result of fairness and justice rather than strict legal ownership and being named on the title deeds.

Figure 8.1 may be helpful to follow when trying to determine how the mortgage has been created.

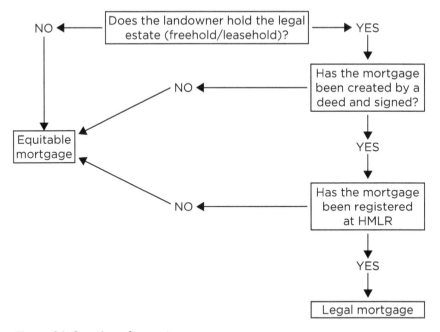

Figure 8.1: Creation of a mortgage

Exam warning

Determining the way in which the mortgage has been created is very important as it will change the remedies available to the mortgagee and the mortgagor for any breach of the mortgage terms. So, do take the time to initially consider this point if the questions requires it.

We shall now consider the enforceability of the mortgage and terms.

ENFORCEABILITY OF MORTGAGE TERMS

When preparing for the SQE1 it is important you understand the enforceability of mortgage terms, which we will consider in two parts – the rights and remedies of the mortgagor and the rights and remedies of the mortgagee.

Rights and remedies of the mortgagor

As we have now established, by granting a mortgage to a lender, the mortgagor is effectively creating a debt secured on their land or property. If the mortgagor defaults on this debt then the mortgagee can take legal action to recover the debt owed to them.

The rights of a mortgagor have changed quite significantly over the years. Prior to 1925 a mortgagor had very few rights when granting a mortgage and common law provisions were not usually favourable to a mortgagor. If a mortgage was required, the mortgagor would convey the whole property or land to the mortgagee and the mortgagee would be considered to be the legal owner of the property. Quite different from today where legal ownership remains with the mortgagor and the mortgagee is named on the title deeds as having a legal charge or interest over the property.

The introduction of the Law of Property Act 1925 sought to establish two ways of creating a legal mortgage, which are by lease or by legal charge (deed) and from this arose the 'equity of redemption' which covers a bundle of rights that the mortgagor will enjoy pending full repayment of the debt.

This included introducing two dates in the lifespan of a mortgage. The first was usually set at six months after the start of the mortgage and this is known as the legal date of redemption. The second date is the end of the mortgage. The time in between the first and second date is known as the **equitable right to redeem**.

> ### Key term: equitable right to redeem
>
> This is the right of a mortgagor to repay the loan in full at any time after the legal date of redemption. This sought to prevent issues that had historically been faced by mortgagors, who, under the common law provisions at the time, would lose all rights to their property if they did not repay the debt by the date of repayment. This prevents mortgagees seeking a power of sale until after the legal date of redemption has passed and also gives the mortgagor the option to repay the mortgage at any time during the equitable right to redeem period if they wanted to do so.

There are several references to 'equity' when discussing mortgages so it is important not to confuse them. The information in **Table 8.1** may help you understand these terms.

Table 8.1: The different references to 'equity'

References to 'equity', which you will need to know as you work through this chapter

Equity of redemption	The bundle of rights the mortgagor holds
Equitable right to redeem	The right of the mortgagor to repay the mortgage in full after the legal redemption date
Equity	The difference between the amount of the mortgage and the value of the property
Negative equity	The amount required to repay the mortgage in full is higher than the value of the property or the sale price

The main benefit of the changes in the mortgagor/mortgagee relationship was it created a contractual one, so an agreement between them both and not a one-sided enforcement of terms from the mortgagee. The law seeks to protect the interests of the mortgagor and allow them to enjoy their land or property without interference from the mortgagee. Once the debt has been repaid in full, also known as **redemption**, the legal interest of the mortgagee can then be removed from the title deeds and the contract comes to an end, the same way as any other debt.

Key term: redemption

This is the process of paying off any outstanding balance owed by the mortgagor to the mortgagee. This is either paid at the end of the mortgage term, in accordance with the terms of the mortgage, or it could be paid off at an earlier date if the mortgagor sells the property. It would then be 'redeemed' from the proceeds of sale.

We shall now consider the range of rights and remedies available to the mortgagor, which are quite broad and fall within a general heading of 'the equity of redemption', as mentioned in **Table 8.1.** There are three main rights which will be considered separately; in brief they are:
- the equitable right to redeem the loan – also known as the doctrine of 'clogs and fetters'
- protection under consumer protection legislation
- protection from undue influence.

The equitable right to redeem – the doctrine of 'clogs and fetters'

A range of issues can fall under this heading but generally it will refer to:
- any unfair conditions in the mortgage. An example would be a term which prevents the mortgagor from fully repaying the mortgage.

- any term that changes the nature of the mortgagor/mortgagee relationship.

Ultimately this doctrine seeks to prevent any unnecessary restrictions or burdens on the mortgagor and allows equity to 'step in', in a variety of different forms, to protect the mortgagor. This is illustrated in **Practice example 8.2**:

Practice example 8.2

David has purchased the property with the mortgage of £106,000 from the Tyne and Wear Building Society. As a term of the mortgage, full repayment (redemption) of the mortgage was restricted from taking place until six weeks before the end of the mortgage term. Would this clause be enforceable, or would it prevent the equitable right to redeem the mortgage?

This is based on the facts in *Fairclough v Swan Brewery* (1912) where it was held that the term was void as it made the right to redeem 'illusionary'. The equitable right to redeem would be ineffective and the mortgage effectively irredeemable. It is also important to note that if there is a clause postponing the right to redeem, but this is not oppressive on the mortgagor or does not completely remove the right to redeem the mortgage, then it may be allowed. The presence of these terms cannot be used as a mechanism by a mortgagor to get out of a mortgage deal that they are no longer happy with.

Exam warning

Just because a clause allowing the mortgagor a right to redeem is present, it does not necessarily make it enforceable. The right needs to be more than simply an 'illusion', it must give the mortgagor something which is clearly beneficial to them.

The other situations where this doctrine may arise would be when the mortgagee is trying to secure **collateral advantage** from the mortgagor, by making it a condition of the mortgage to only purchase products, such as insurance, from the mortgagee. However, it is important to note that equity will only step in and allow the court to set aside any collateral conditions where they are unconscionable, so it can be shown that they are morally wrong. There is nothing to prohibit these types of terms within mortgage conditions where they are conscionable and do not last beyond the point when the mortgage is redeemed.

Key term: collateral advantage

A situation where one of the contracting parties (usually the mortgagee) uses their stronger bargaining position or power to agree the mortgage on terms that are far more favourable to them.

Protection under consumer protection legislation

Where there does appear to be a significant imbalance of rights between the mortgagor and mortgagee, the mortgagor can also potentially rely upon consumer protection legislation. It is important to know this for the SQE because whilst consumer protection legislation does not have a significant impact on the legal advice you can give to a client in a practical example (as solicitors are usually not regulated to provide financial advice), it is important to note it here so that you are aware of it and how the mortgagor should be given sufficient information to ensure they are fully aware of the risks associated with mortgage conditions. The legislation available can be separated out as follows:

- Consumer Rights Act 2015, which will govern general unfair terms
- Financial Service and Markets Act 2000, this applies to mortgages created after 31 October 2004 and stipulates that those providing regulated mortgage contracts must ensure they are fair and transparent. Failure to do so could result in a claim for compensation from the mortgagor.
- Consumer Credit Act 2006 allows the courts to intervene if they find the mortgagor/mortgagee relationship to be unfair on the mortgagor.

Protection from undue influence

Equity will also intervene on the side of a mortgagor where there is evidence of undue influence being exerted by one side over the other. The doctrine of **undue influence** is a difficult one as, if proven, it can result in the entire mortgage being set aside. As such, the courts must weigh up the interests of the mortgagee and the protection of the mortgagor in a situation that usually, but not always, arises as a result of the mortgagor's actions.

Key term: undue influence

A decision made by a person without their free will due to pressure exerted upon them by another.

Practice example 8.3 outlines a typical scenario which will help to explain this further.

Practice example 8.3

Carlos owns a property with Nicholas, which they own in law and equity as joint tenants. Carlos needs to raise some money quickly for a business deal and so asks Nicholas to agree to a mortgage on their property. Nicholas is reluctant but Carlos assures him that this is a short-term loan and is limited to £30,000. Nicholas reluctantly agrees and the mortgagee is aware of the fact that the mortgage was to finance Carlos' business deal. The mortgagee writes to Nicholas to advise him to seek independent legal advice but they do not check that he has done this, nor does the letter explain any of the implication of the additional loan. Nicholas does not read the letter. Carlos defaults on the mortgage two months later and it transpires that the mortgage was for £100,000 over a term of 15 years. The mortgagee is now threatening legal action against them both. Can Nicholas rely on undue influence in this situation?

This is based on the facts in *Barclays Bank v O'Brien* [1993] where the court agreed to set aside the mortgage on the basis of the bank's constructive notice of Mr O'Brien's misrepresentation of the scope and nature of the mortgage. It was held that the bank failed to take reasonable steps to ensure that Mrs O'Brien was fully aware of the nature and consequences of the mortgage.

We will now consider the ways in which undue influence can occur.

Proving undue influence

The O'Brien case mentioned above set out two main categories of undue influence. Those being:

- presumed undue influence and
- actual undue influence.

Presumed undue influence could arise in relationships where one party could have influence over another person who may be vulnerable, such as, doctor–patient, solicitor–client. It is presumed that a client would trust and act on the advice of their solicitor and so they could claim undue influence if there has been a breach of that trust. For example, a solicitor who encourages a client to appoint them as the only trustee in the client's will, knowing they will then be able to make more fees from the probate, could be shown to unduly influence the client for their own benefit.

It could also arise if there is evidence of a relationship of trust and confidence and the transaction called for an explanation. **Practice example 8.4** will explain this further.

Practice example 8.4

Yiannis purchased a property with his mother in joint names. Several years later Yiannis needed money for a business venture and a second mortgage was granted to North East Mortgages. Yiannis' mother does not read English but signed the relevant documentation to consent to the second mortgage (she has trust and confidence in her son). The legal documents were not read to her. Yiannis then defaulted on the mortgage and North East Mortgages wish to repossess the property. Could Yiannis' mother claim presumed undue influence by her son to set aside the second mortgage?

These are the facts of *Abbey National plc v Stringer* (2006) in which the court agreed that the relationship between the mother and son could be construed as one of trust and confidence. The terms of the mortgage should have been explained to the mother. The result of this was that the mother was entitled to the entire beneficial interest in the property.

For a claim of *actual undue influence* to be successful the claimant must be able to point to specific evidence and positively prove that they have been subject to undue influence to enter into the mortgage. This could easily be something which you are tested on as part of the SQE. In a case of actual undue influence, it can be quite difficult to prove exactly what was said between the two parties.

However, proving that undue influence exists will not automatically mean that the mortgage will be set aside. The case of *Royal Bank of Scotland v Etridge* (no.2) [2001] established various steps the mortgagee can take to protect themselves if undue influence is established. This is also known as the Etridge Protocol and is as follows:

a) Is there proof of undue influence?

b) Was the mortgagee aware of the relationship of the mortgagor and so was 'put on inquiry'? This will arise if the mortgagee is aware that one party is acting as a guarantee for the other party's debt, and the loan is for the sole benefit of that other party.

c) If so, did the mortgagee take reasonable steps to minimise the risk of undue influence arising. Case law has developed a comprehensive list of steps the bank should take if they are 'put on inquiry'. Some of these are:

- Did the mortgagee state that any third party should seek independent legal advice?
- If the same solicitor is being used by both parties, did the mortgagee ask whether the party claiming undue influence wishes to instruct a different solicitor?
- The mortgagee should provide the solicitor instructed with all relevant financial information, such as debts, purpose and amount of the mortgage and any suspicion of undue influence it may have.
- Independent legal advice must be given by the solicitor to the party claiming undue influence.
- The solicitor must provide the mortgagee with evidence of the advice given.

Figure 8.2 should be helpful in answering a question of this type.

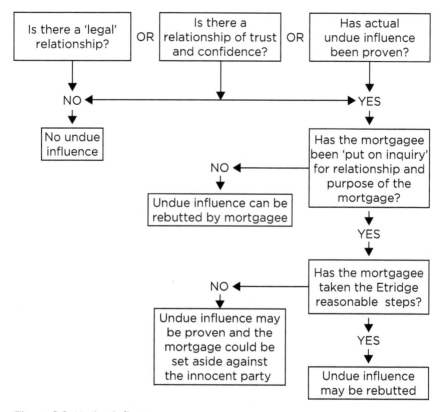

Figure 8.2: Undue influence

Rights and remedies of the mortgagee

We now need to consider the rights and remedies of the mortgagee for non-payment of the mortgage or default on any terms and conditions. Again, these can be set out in the following broad categories:

• the right to payment
• the right to possession
• power of sale
• appointing a receiver
• foreclosure.

It is important to note that the mortgagee is not actually obliged to take any of the above remedies, but if they do then there are certain duties they will still owe to the mortgagor, which we will consider below. If they do decide to take a particular remedy, but it is unsuccessful, they can then simply move on to the next remedy until the debt is satisfied; the remedies can be used singularly or cumulatively.

We will consider these remedies in turn below.

The right to payment

Contractual liability is central to the relationship between a mortgagor and mortgagee. As with any contract, if a term is breached the injured party can sue on the contract. So, if the mortgagor does not pay the agreed monthly payments, then the mortgagee can sue for repayment.

This remedy has both positives and negatives for the mortgagee. The negatives are that if the mortgagor cannot pay the monthly repayments then it is unlikely they will be able to pay following any court hearing. The positives are that being a contractual debt, the mortgagee can continue to pursue for the debt even if the property is sold and there is a shortfall; this is referred to as 'negative equity', which we considered within **Table 8.1** and means that the mortgagor owes more to the lender than what the property has been sold for.

This remedy is usually used in conjunction with the right to possession or a power of sale. **Practice example 8.5** explains this further.

Practice example 8.5

David has fallen into arrears with his monthly repayments to the Tyne and Wear Building Society. The mortgagee has started court action to recover the debt and seeks a power of sale, both of which are granted by the court. When the court order is made David still owes £100,000. The property is sold for £90,000, meaning there is still a debt of £10,000 owed to the mortgagee. Can the mortgagee recover this shortfall?

Tyne and Wear Building Society, under the contractual action, have a 12-year period in which to recover this outstanding debt but only six years to recover any interest owed.

The right to possession

As with the right to payment, the right to possession usually arises in situations where there is a default by the mortgagor on the mortgage payments.

The mortgagee may wish to seek possession in advance of seeking an order of sale to ensure the property is vacant before it is sold. They may also seek possession to manage the property and generate an income to satisfy the mortgagor's debts. The latter is unlikely in residential property as the mortgagee is usually not interested in possessing the property.

There are a number of important duties or limits, placed upon the mortgagee if they intend to seek possession; these are:
- complying with s 6(1) Criminal Law Act 1977 which specifies that possession of land should not be undertaken without the order of the court
- limitations of s 36 Administration of Justice Act 1970; this potentially provides the mortgagor with a lifeline if they can demonstrate to the court that they have a realistic prospect of repaying the debts. If so, the court has the ability to delay the possession proceedings for a reasonable period – see **Practice example 8.6**.
- the court's inherent jurisdiction to postpone possession; whilst the courts do have the power to postpone possession in accordance with s 36 AJA, they are also able to grant temporary relief under a broad equitable jurisdiction, to a mortgagor in arrears. This, however, would usually be very limited, to a number of weeks at most. This inherent jurisdiction to postpone would not apply if the property is in negative equity.
- limitations of Family Law Act 1996 in protection of spousal rights; again, this provides the court with the power to postpone possession if there is a **connected person** who should be made party

to the proceedings. This is likely to happen where a cohabitee has contributed towards the mortgage or where a spouse has registered their occupational rights under the Matrimonial Homes Act 1983. This will allow the connected person to play a more active role in the proceedings and possibly persuade a court to postpone possession if they can demonstrate they are able to satisfy the debts.

Key term: connected person

S 54(5) Family Law Act 1996 defines a connected person as a spouse, former spouse, civil partner, former civil partner, cohabitant or former cohabitant. This would allow those persons to become a party to the proceedings and ask to postpone proceedings.

Practice example 8.6

David has fallen into arrears with his monthly repayments to the Tyne and Wear Building Society. The mortgagee has started court action for possession proceedings and to seek a power of sale. David defends this on the basis that he can repay the arrears within a reasonable period. He produces evidence which explains that he has accumulated the arrears due to an injury at work which stopped him working and as he is self-employed, he was not entitled to any benefits. He has recently returned to work and has started paying off the arrears. He is hopeful to have all arrears paid within six months. Are the courts likely to use their power under s 36 AJA to postpone possession?

This is based on the facts of *Cheltenham & Gloucester Building Society v Norgan* [1996], where the court proposed certain considerations that are relevant when looking at exercising discretion to postpone proceedings. These include, how much the mortgagor can afford to repay, whether any temporary difficulties in meeting repayments will be resolved quickly, the reasons for the arrears and what the relevant contractual terms are.

Power of sale

This remedy is almost always used in connection with the right to possession because it is usually easier to sell properties by a mortgagee when the property is vacant. Most mortgage deeds will now always contain an express power of sale to the mortgagee; however, they can

still exercise this remedy if no express clause is made under the statutory powers granted under LPA 1925. This is a twofold test. Firstly, the power of sale must 'arise', which it does when the following conditions are met:
- the mortgage is made by a deed
- the **legal date of redemption** has passed, which will be specified in the mortgage conditions but is usually six months from the date that the mortgage was created
- there is no clause expressly excluding the power of sale.

Key term: legal date of redemption

This is a term which specifies a date when the mortgagor *can* repay the mortgage, not that they *must* pay it at this date.

Once the power of sale has *arisen,* the mortgagee can enforce the same if the following conditions are met:
- notice of any default has been served to the mortgagor and three months have elapsed without full payment of the debt OR
- some interest under the mortgage is in arrears and unpaid for two months after becoming due OR
- there has been a breach of any other term of the mortgage.

So, you will note that only one of these conditions needs to be met for the power of sale to arise. Consider **Practice example 8.7** for more information on this provision.

Practice example 8.7

David has now owned his property for two years. He has recently defaulted on three payments on the mortgage with the Tyne and Wear Building Society. He receives a letter from them demanding repayment of all arrears immediately. Three months have passed and he has not repaid the full arrears, only some of it. Can the mortgagee now exercise its power of sale?

Yes, from the facts we can see that the power of sale has arisen as the legal date of redemption has passed and we can assume, unless told otherwise, that the mortgage is made by deed and does not exclude the power of sale. David has defaulted, he has received notice of this, three months have passed and he has not repaid all the debt, so the power of sale is now exercisable and the mortgagee can legally sell David's home.

It is worth noting that there is no need for the mortgagee to obtain a court order for sale in this way, but they would usually apply for the right to possession as detailed earlier in the chapter.

Concerns around abuse of power of the mortgagee have arisen over the years and so certain obligations are placed on mortgagees in this position, which have been developed by case law. These obligations are:

- duty to act in good faith, which means they must conduct an honest sale to an unconnected person. They cannot sell the property to themselves or to nominees in trust for themselves
- obtaining the true market value. A mortgagee cannot simply sell the property at any price it wants to, or at an undervalue just to ensure their debt is paid off. They have a duty to obtain the true market value of the property. See **Practice example 8.8** for an illustration of this.
- timing and mode of sale. The mortgagee is generally able to exercise its discretion as to when it sells the property and does not have to wait until market conditions improve, but it still maintains that duty to obtain a proper price for the land. They can also choose how to sell, whether by public auction or by selling on the open market but must ensure the full information about the property is made available to prospective purchasers.

If a mortgagee fails to comply with these obligations then the mortgagor could seek a court order for the sale to be set aside or that the mortgagee pay for any shortfall in the sale price and the price that could have been obtained for the land.

Practice example 8.8

Following events in **Practice example 8.7**, a power of sale has arisen and is now exercisable. David informs the bank that the property has planning permission granted for a two-storey extension, loft conversion and rear extension, all of which would increase the value of the land to around £130,000. The mortgagee decides to sell the property at auction but only the single storey rear extension is mentioned and the property sells for £120,000. Did the mortgagee have a duty to ensure the correct information was published in connection with the sale?

Yes. This is based on the facts of *Cuckmere Brick Co. v Mutual Finance* (1971) where failure to fully publicise that the land had

planning permission to build 100 flats meant the land sold for £31,000 less than it was valued at. Mutual Finance had breached its duty to act in good faith, to take reasonable care in conducting the sale and to obtain a fair and proper price for the land. The mortgagee was required to compensate the mortgagor for the shortfall.

Appointing a receiver

A mortgagee would usually look to this remedy in commercial premises. The receiver would be appointed to take over the management of the property or premises, so receiving the rental income, paying any associated expenses and paying any surplus back to the mortgagee. These are seldom used in residential transactions due to the possible costs involved in managing the property, such as paying any expenses which are unlikely to be recoverable.

Foreclosure

This remedy is very rarely used and there have been recommendations by the Law Commission to abolish it completely. This remedy has the effect of completely extinguishing the mortgagor's equity of redemption. If the debt is not paid off in full by a certain date the whole of the property then vests in the mortgagee and they can become the registered proprietors of the property. The mortgagee also does not have to pay the mortgagor any increased value in the property over the amount of the mortgage, which is why the courts are very unlikely to grant foreclosure in cases where the value of the property is in excess of the mortgage debt. It should be noted that this provision only applies to foreclosure.

Despite this, it is a rather unattractive remedy for most mortgagees, especially in cases of negative equity as it also extinguishes any rights for the mortgagee to sue for any shortfall in the mortgage.

Other points to consider

The pre-action protocol was introduced in November 2008 and applies to all mortgagees who hold a first legal charge over residential properties. This means they have the priority charge shown in the title deeds. The aim of the protocol is to reduce litigation wherever possible. This will include having an open dialog between the mortgagor and mortgagee and if possible, agreeing payment plans where suitable.

It is also worth noting that, once the power of sale is exercised, the mortgagee then has the following obligations in repayment of the proceeds of sale:

a) firstly, to repay any prior mortgages (if any)

b) then to repay any costs, charges or expenses occurred in selling the property, so solicitors or selling agent fees

c) to pay any sums owed to the mortgagee who sold the property, including capital and interest

d) to pay any balance remaining to any subsequent mortgagees; if there are none then to the mortgagor. This will be explained further when we consider the priority of mortgages.

Figure 8.3 may help when considering the actions of a mortgagee should you receive a question of this type in the exam.

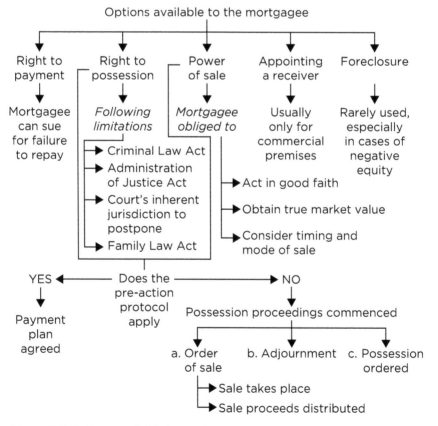

Figure 8.3: Options available to mortgagee

It is also necessary for us to consider the priority of mortgages as that will also determine some of the rights and remedies available to the mortgagee.

THE PRIORITY OF MORTGAGES

It is possible to have more than one mortgage secured against a property and when repaying these mortgages, it must be done in a certain order.

Where the sale price is sufficient to meet the full amount of all mortgages there is usually no issue when a property is sold. However, you could be asked about where there is a shortfall, or a negative equity situation in the SQE; then you need to consider the priority of mortgages, with some differences between equitable and legal charges and registered and unregistered land. We will consider legal charges first and **Practice example 8.9** should help explain this further.

Practice example 8.9

David granted a mortgage to the Tyne and Wear Building Society on the 18th May 2017 and this was registered with HM Land Registry on the 9th June 2017. Tyne and Wear Building Society hold the first legal charge over the property. David grants a second mortgage to Seaham Shore Bank on the 25th October 2019 which is registered with HM Land Registry on the 17th November 2019. Seaham Shore Bank hold a second, or subsequent legal charge over the property. In April 2020 David loses his job and misses some repayments on both mortgages. Tyne and Wear Building Society obtain a power of sale and sell the property for £120,000. A sum of £110,000 remains outstanding under the mortgage to Tyne and Wear Building Society and a sum of £25,000 remains outstanding to Seaham Shore Bank. How will the proceeds of sale be split when considering the priority of the mortgagees?

All legal charges must be registered in the charges register of the title deeds (Chapter 4) and they will take priority *in order of the date they are registered*, not when they are created. So, a delay in registration of a mortgage could have quite disastrous consequences in the case of negative equity. However, in this example, Tyne and Wear Building Society can discharge the full mortgage amount owed to them and there would be £10,000

> left for Seaham Shore Bank. Seaham Shore Bank would then
> need to seek a further action against David if they wanted to
> try and reclaim the balance of £15,000 owed to them under the
> contract.

Equitable mortgages

Practice example 8.9 shows how the priority of mortgages works when dealing with legal mortgages. This differs from equitable mortgages because equitable mortgages are either granted by a mortgagor with an equitable ownership in the land or where there is legal ownership but the deed has not been completed or registered correctly.

There are also some important differences to consider for the priority of equitable mortgages when dealing with registered or unregistered land, both of which have different systems of establishing whether equitable mortgages are binding on future purchasers.

Registered land

To ensure priority of an equitable mortgage in registered land it must be protected by way of a notice on the title deeds (**Chapter 4**). When equitable mortgages are protected in this way that mortgagee will take priority over any later mortgagee.

Unregistered land

When dealing with unregistered land it is usual for the first mortgagee to have control of the title deeds and this effectively prevents the mortgagor from any further dealings with the land, including granting any subsequent mortgages. Depositing the title deeds with a mortgagee in this way would be sufficient evidence of an equitable mortgage.

Following the introduction of the Law of Property (Miscellaneous Provisions) Act 1989, depositing deeds with the mortgagee was not sufficient evidence of an equitable mortgage since all interests in land had to be created by a deed. As such, any subsequent equitable mortgages must now be protected by registration of a C(i) land charge (**Chapter 3**) and if this is done then it will take priority over all later interests. If it is not, then that mortgage will be void against any future purchaser for valuable consideration.

Look at **Figure 8.4** which will explain this further.

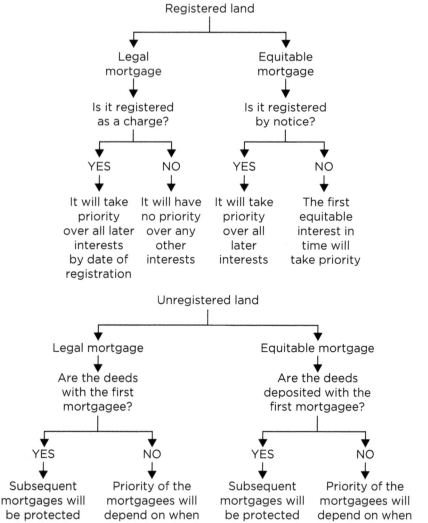

Figure 8.4: Priority of mortgagees

Tacking

An important consideration when looking at priority of mortgagees is **tacking**. It is very common for mortgagors, rather than granting mortgages to various mortgagees, to simply ask the original mortgagee to provide a further loan, in addition to the original loan. So, it is 'tacked' onto the existing agreement.

Key term: tacking

Tacking means to lend further money under an original mortgage agreement.

Tacking can cause two problems:
- Those mortgagees with priority mortgages may not recover all the outstanding loan amount if they have received notice of a subsequent mortgage.
- Those with subsequent mortgages may not recover all their outstanding loan amount if they do not check whether the priority mortgagee has granted any further advances.

Look at **Practice example 8.10** which explains this further.

Practice example 8.10

David currently owes £100,000 on the mortgage agreement with Tyne and Wear Building Society. He then gets into financial difficulties and Tyne and Wear Building Society sell the property for £120,000. Prior to his financial difficulties, David
1) granted a further mortgage against the property in favour of Seaham Shore Bank for the sum of £25,000
2) subsequently obtained a further loan advance from Tyne and Wear Building Society for an amount of £10,000.

Tyne and Wear Building Society are owed £110,000 collectively on the mortgage agreement. Which mortgagee has priority over the other and how much can they recover?

If Seaham Shore Bank had agreed to the 'tacking' of this further advance by Tyne and Wear Building Society then the full £110,000 would go to Tyne and Wear Building Society and Seaham Shore Bank would only be able to recover £10,000 of their outstanding loan.

If, however, Seaham Shore Bank were not aware or did not agree to the further advance then £100,000 would be paid to Tyne and Wear Building Society in respect to the original mortgage amount,

£20,000 would be paid to Seaham Shore Bank. Both would then need to seek a further action against David if they wanted to try and reclaim the balance owed to them under the separate contracts.

■ KEY POINT CHECKLIST

This chapter has covered the following key knowledge points. You can use these to structure your revision around, making sure to recall the key details for each point, as covered in this chapter.

- You must be clear on who the mortgagor and the mortgagee are as there are different rights and remedies available to both parties. The mortgagor is the person granting the mortgage, so the legal owner of the land. The mortgagee is the company or individual loaning money to another individual in return for an interest in the land.
- Whilst most mortgages are legal in nature, so created by a deed and registered, you must also be aware of how equitable mortgages are created which will arise where an individual owns an equitable interest in land or where there is a defective legal mortgage.
- There are various rights and remedies available to a mortgagor. These are, the right to enjoy the land or property without interference from the mortgagee, the equitable right to redeem, known as the doctrine of 'clogs and fetters', protection under consumer protection legislation and protection from undue influence by other mortgagors.
- There are also various rights and remedies available to a mortgagee. These are, the right to payment, the right to possession, the right to request a power of sale, the right to appoint a receiver and the option of foreclosure, which is seldom used in residential mortgages.
- You will need to be aware of the priority of mortgages and how this will affect the rights and remedies of the mortgagee where there is more than one. This will include being aware of whether any additional mortgage sums have been 'tacked' onto an existing mortgage which could change the priority of repayment.

■ KEY TERMS AND CONCEPTS

- mortgagor (**page 184**)
- mortgagee (**page 184**)
- equitable interest (**page 186**)
- equitable right to redeem (**page 188**)
- redemption (**page 189**)
- collateral advantage (**page 190**)
- undue influence (**page 191**)

- connected person (**page 196**)
- legal date of redemption (**page 198**)
- tacking (**page 204**)

■ SQE1-STYLE QUESTIONS

QUESTION 1

A client has sought legal advice as she is purchasing a property and is granting a mortgage in the sum of £185,000 to a local bank. The mortgage terms and conditions include the following condition: 'the redemption of this mortgage can take place at any time once six months from the creation of the mortgage, but it must be redeemed by the mortgagor only'.

Which of the following reflects the best advice to provide about this term?

A. That this is a general mortgage term to protect the interest of the mortgagee.

B. That this is a valid term as the mortgagee has confirmed that the equitable right to redeem applies.

C. This term would be invalid and unenforceable because it is an unfair term.

D. This term would be considered a 'clog and fetter' as it is unreasonable in its nature and there should be no restrictions on the right to redeem.

E. This term would be considered a 'clog and fetter' as the mortgagee is trying to gain a collateral advantage from the mortgagor.

QUESTION 2

A mortgage company has tried to commence repossession proceedings for non-payment of the mortgage against the mortgagor, who are a husband and wife. The wife has claimed undue influence by her husband and that she was unaware of the nature or extent of the mortgage. The mortgage money was used by the husband to try and raise money in stocks and shares. This was unsuccessful and they have now defaulted on the mortgage payments. The mortgage application stated that the purpose of the mortgage was to purchase a second property as a holiday home for both mortgagors.

Which of the following best reflects the wife's legal position in relation to the possession application?

A. The wife can rely upon undue influence as there is a clear relationship of trust and confidence between the wife and her husband.

B. The wife can rely upon undue influence as there is a clear legal relationship between the wife and her husband.

C. Whilst there is a relationship of trust and confidence between the wife and her husband, the mortgagee was not put on notice as to the true purpose of the mortgage and so the undue influence can be rebutted.

D. The wife can rely upon presumed undue influence as there is a clear relationship of trust and confidence between the wife and her husband.

E. Whilst there is a relationship of trust and confidence between the wife and her husband, the mortgagee sent all the necessary legal documents to the mortgagors and so the undue influence can be rebutted.

QUESTION 3

A client has sought legal advice. The client and her partner both live in the same property but her partner is the legal and equitable owner. The client has lived in the property since it was purchased and has always contributed to the mortgage and other significant works to the property, such as a recent extension. The client has discovered that her partner has fallen behind with the mortgage payments and there is a court hearing next week where the mortgagee is looking to take possession of the property. The client wants to stop this and has said that she will pay the mortgage and the arrears. The client is in full time employment and can afford to do this.

Which of the following best represents the legal position of the client?

A. The client can ask the court to make her a party to the proceedings as a connected person. This will allow her to try and persuade the court to delay the proceedings.

B. The proceedings will not be stopped as the court have no inherent jurisdiction to postpone any proceedings of this kind.

C. The client can show that she is able to repay the mortgage in a reasonable time and so the proceedings would be postponed.

D. The client can ask the court to consider that the mortgagee has not followed correct procedures and can ask them to postpone the proceedings as she will be extremely distraught if the property is repossessed.

E. The client is not a legal owner of the property and so the court will not allow her to be involved in the proceedings in any way.

QUESTION 4

A mortgage company have recently taken possession of a residential property. They are owed £150,000 under the mortgage agreement. The property is a listed building and they have been made aware that there is valid planning and conservation area permission on the property for a full renovation, meaning the property is worth around £200,000. The mortgage company list the property with an online auction but fail to mention the relevant permissions that have been granted and they obtain £152,000 for the property, which they are very happy with as it means their mortgage is repaid in full and there is enough to cover the legal costs. The mortgagor is unhappy with this and wants advice.

Which of the following best represents the mortgagor's legal position?

A. It is very unfortunate situation for the mortgagor, but the mortgage company cannot predict the property market in this way, and they are only able to sell the property for what someone is willing to pay for it.

B. The mortgage company has done nothing wrong here, they have acted in good faith as they have sold the property to an unconnected person.

C. The mortgage company only has an obligation to recover enough to repay the mortgage and the mortgagor should be happy with this otherwise they could have exercised their contractual rights to recover any shortfall had there been any.

D. The mortgage company should not have listed the property with an online auction agent. This has breached their duty of care to the mortgagor. The mortgagor can sue the mortgage company for the £48,000 difference.

E. The mortgage company had a duty to obtain a true market value of the property by providing all the relevant information to the auction agent. They may be in breach of this duty and the mortgagor could look to seek compensation between the amount received and what could have reasonably been achieved for the property.

QUESTION 5

A client currently owes £122,000 on a mortgage agreement with Number 1 Bank. She then grants a further mortgage in favour of Number 2 Bank, on which she currently owes £32,000. She then grants a further mortgage in favour of Number 3 Bank, on which she currently owes £5,000. The client is now unable to pay any of the mortgage agreements and Number 2 Bank seek possession proceedings and an order to sell the property, which they are granted and recover the true market value of the property which was £150,000.

Which of the following best reflects the advice you would give in relation to how these mortgages would be repaid?

A. Number 2 Bank would be required to repay the entirety of their loan first as they are the ones who sought the court orders and sold the property.

B. Number 2 Bank would be required to repay all prior mortgages and then any costs and fees associated with the sale before paying their own mortgage.

C. Number 2 Bank would be required to repay the entirety of their loan first as they are the ones who sought the court orders and sold the property; they would then repay Number 3 Bank as theirs is the smallest mortgage amount and Number 1 Bank would receive the surplus.

D. Number 2 Bank would be required to pay £122,000 to Number 1 Bank, then £28,000 to themselves. Number 3 Bank and anyone else owed money, such as the solicitors or selling agents, would have to sue under a personal contract to recover their money.

E. Number 2 Bank would be required to repay all mortgagees an equal sum proportionate to the value of their loan amount; they must leave enough to pay all associated fees and disbursements.

■ ANSWERS TO QUESTIONS

Answers to 'What do you know already?' questions at the start of the chapter

1) The correct answer was B. A legal mortgage must always be recorded on the title deeds.

2) The correct answer was true. The person who grants the mortgage is the mortgagor; they grant the mortgage and the legal interest in their land to the mortgagee.

3) The correct answer was C. All the other answers are rights available to the mortgagor.

4) The correct answer was D. They would need to demonstrate that they are connected in some way for the court to consider joining them to the proceedings.

5) The correct answer was E. There are certain conditions that must have been met before the mortgagee can use the power of sale. Those are that there is a legal mortgage, the legal date of redemption has passed and there is no clause that excludes a power of sale.

Answers to end-of-chapter SQE1-style assessment questions

Question 1:

The correct answer was D. This is because the clause could potentially make the mortgage irredeemable. If, for example, the client died she would never be able to repay the mortgage personally, therefore making the mortgage term unreasonable. A and B are incorrect as this is not or should not be a standard general or valid term. Whilst C may be a valid option for the client, unfair terms are generally governed by consumer protection legislation which may be outside the scope of advice a solicitor is permitted to give. E is incorrect as a collateral advantage is where the mortgagee tries to tie the client into some financial payments for the mortgagee's own benefit, such as insisting they take out life insurance with the mortgagee.

Question 2:

The correct answer was C. This is because whilst there is clearly a relationship of trust and confidence between husband and wife, the mortgagee did not know the true purpose of the mortgage and so they were not put on notice of the possible equitable interest of the wife and so could not take sufficient steps to protect themselves. A is incorrect as it does not go far enough in the scope of advice as with option C. B is incorrect as this is not an example of a legal relationship. D is incorrect as a relationship with presumed undue influence usually arises with a doctor–patient, solicitor–client relationship. E is incorrect as the undue influence can be rebutted if they take full steps to protect themselves, and just sending documents to the wife would not be sufficient.

Question 3:

The correct answer was A. This is because the client is the partner of the mortgagor and this would allow her to apply to become a party to the proceedings and ask to postpone proceedings. B and E are incorrect as the court do have inherent jurisdiction to postpone any proceedings or add a third party to the proceedings. C and D are incorrect as those would ordinarily be options available to the original mortgagor, not the third party.

Question 4:

The correct answer was E. This is because when a mortgagee is granted a power of sale they have a legal obligation to obtain the true market value of the property. A mortgagee cannot simply sell the property at any price it wants to, or at an undervalue just to ensure their debt is paid off, which is why options A, B and C are incorrect. Option D is incorrect as there is no restriction on placing the property on the market with an online only agent.

Question 5:

The correct answer was B. This is because under the power of sale it specifies that all mortgages must be repaid in the order in which they were registered. So, those that are registered first in the title deeds must be repaid first, then the selling costs and then the balance to any other mortgagees who have a registered legal charge, which is why options D and E are incorrect. A and C are incorrect as Number 2 Bank are second in line with the registered mortgages and so Number 1 Bank have priority over them.

■ KEY CASES, RULES, STATUTES AND INSTRUMENTS

The SQE1 Assessment Specification does not require you to know any case names, or statutory materials, for the topic of land law. Despite this, you may find it useful to become familiar with these statutes:

Administration of Justice Act 1970

Consumer Credit Act 2006

Consumer Rights Act 2015

Criminal Law Act 1977

Financial Service and Markets Act 2000

Law of Property (Miscellaneous Provisions) Act 1989

Law of Property Act 1925

Land Registration Act 2002

Matrimonial Homes Act 1983.

9

Co-ownership

■ MAKE SURE YOU KNOW

This chapter will focus on the key elements of the differences between joint tenants and tenants in common in law and in equity, what happens to the co-ownership when one of the owners dies, how to change the co-ownership and how to solve disagreements between co-owners by reference to sections 14 and 15 of Trusts of Land & Appointment of Trustees Act 1996. This will enable you to tackle any SQE1 questions on this topic.

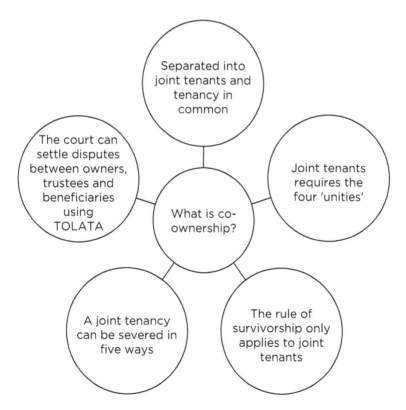

■ SQE ASSESSMENT ADVICE

As you work through this chapter, remember to pay particular attention in your revision to:
- differences between joint tenants and tenants in common, both in law and in equity
- rule of survivorship
- severance of joint tenancies
- solving disagreements between co-owners.

■ WHAT DO YOU KNOW ALREADY?

Try answering these questions before reading this chapter. If you find some difficult or can't remember the answers, make a note to look more closely at that subtopic during your revision.

1) True or false? Only the unity of possession is required to prove a joint tenancy.

   [What is co-ownership?, page 215]

2) What is the correct position of a tenancy in common?
   a) Both the legal and equitable title in the property are owned collectively by all owners.
   b) The legal title is held in unequal shares.
   c) The equitable title is held by one party only.
   d) The legal title is owned collectively by the owners and the equitable title can be held in unequal shares.
   e) Only the court can determine the existence of a tenancy in common.

   [What is co-ownership?, page 215]

3) An unmarried couple own a property as joint tenants in equity and law. Person 1 paid £10,000 towards the purchase price and person 2 paid £45,000. What is the correct position if the property is to be sold and sale proceeds split between them?
   a) They will both receive their original contributions and any further equity will be split 50/50.
   b) They will receive 50% each, regardless of their original contributions.
   c) They will both receive their original contributions and any further equity will be split as a percentage in accordance with their original contributions.
   d) Only the court can determine the split of any proceeds of sale between the parties.

e) The full sale proceeds will be paid to person 2 as they made the highest contribution to the purchase price.

[Tenancy in common, page 219]

4) Abbie and Wilson are friends and they own a property together as tenants in common. Wilson owns an 80% share and Abbie a 20% share. Abbie dies in a tragic accident but does not have a Will.

What will happen to Abbie's share in the property?

a) Wilson will become trustee for any beneficiary that may be identified and he has a duty to hold any trust funds until a beneficiary is identified.

b) Wilson will have to sell the property and transfer 20% of the sale proceeds over to the crown within 12 months of Abbie's death.

c) As there is no Will, the property will now transfer to Wilson and he will become the sole legal owner.

d) Wilson will now own the property on his own and the full legal and equitable title will be in his sole name.

e) Wilson will become trustee for any beneficiary that may be identified and he cannot sell the property until a beneficiary is found.

[Tenancy in common, page 219]

5) True or false? If there is a dispute between co-owners, beneficiaries or trustees and a claim is made under s 15 TOLATA, the court only ever need to have consideration of the original intention of the parties before making an order for sale.

[Solving disputes between co-owners under TOLATA 1996, page 223]

WHAT IS CO-OWNERSHIP?

When land or property is purchased by more than one individual, they have a choice to make on how they will own or 'hold' the legal and equitable title to that land or property.

There are two types of co-ownership, those being **joint tenancy** and **tenancy in common**.

> **Key term: joint tenancy**
>
> Joint tenancy is where both the legal and the equitable title in the property are owned collectively as a whole by all owners.

> ### Key term: tenancy in common
>
> Tenancy in common is where the legal title only is owned collectively as a whole by all owners but the equitable title can be owned in equal or unequal shares.

There are some very important differences between the two forms of co-ownership so this chapter will start by looking at those as follows.

Joint tenancy

This is usually the easier of the two forms of co-ownership and means that all of the owners own the land collectively. There is no separation of ownership, no one will own a specific share in the land or property. Even where the owners may have contributed to the purchase price in unequal amounts, if there is an express declaration of a joint tenancy then that is how the land or property will be owned. Both the **legal title** and the **equitable title** will be owned jointly by the parties (**Chapter 1**).

> ### Key term: legal title
>
> Legal title means the owners in law, the names shown on the paper title deeds. They have the right to sell the property.

> ### Key term: equitable title
>
> Equitable title means the owners have the right to benefit from the property, by living in it, receiving rent or receiving sale proceeds when it is sold.

Practice example 9.1 gives an example of joint tenancy in practice.

> ### Practice example 9.1
>
> Robert and Irenna both own their property, which they purchased for £185,000. Irenna contributed £25,000 to the purchase and Rob contributed £5,000. The balance was obtained by granting a mortgage to a local mortgage company. Within the purchase deed both Robert and Irenna made an express declaration that they wished to own the property as joint tenants.

The property is sold for £200,000. After paying the balance of the mortgage of £150,000 what will happen to the remaining sale proceeds? Will Robert and Irenna receive their initial contributions and the remainder be split between them?

No. There was an express declaration of joint tenancy and so the sale proceeds would be split equally, regardless of the initial contributions made by the parties. They both own the legal and the equitable title to the property meaning they would both receive £25,000 following the sale.

Revision tip

Try not to confuse the word 'tenant' or 'tenancy' in this chapter to the modern day use of this word, which relates to someone renting a property or having a lease over land as discussed in **Chapter 5**. Tenancy or tenant in this context relates to the historical use of this word which ultimately means to own or hold an estate in land.

There are two distinguishing features of joint tenancy, those are:
- the four unities
- the right of survivorship.

The four unities
The first of the two features required for a joint tenancy is that the parties have the 'four unities', which are:
- unity of possession: this has been considered briefly in the first example, it relates to all owners of the land or property being able to use and enjoy every piece of it collectively. There are no dividing barriers or restrictions on use by one party to another.
- unity of interest: this means that each co-owner must have identical rights in the land or property. If they are both registered as the owners of the freehold land then this will be satisfied. If, for example, one party owned the freehold interest and the other the leasehold interest, they would own separate estates in the land and so could not have unity of interest.
- unity of title: this means that the co-owners must have acquired their title in the same way, so by the same transaction and by the same document.
- unity of time: similar to unity of title, but each co-owner must have acquired their interest at the same time. In situations where there is a

conditional gift, eg, siblings or other relatives obtaining the property upon reaching a certain age, then unless they are born on the same day this would mean this condition is not satisfied.

Where one of these unities is not present, and in the absence of an express declaration, then the property will not be owned as a joint tenancy but rather as a tenancy in common.

The right of survivorship

The other very important feature of a joint tenancy is the right of survivorship. As stated above, the co-owners do not own their own separate or distinguished share of the property and as such, if one co-owner dies, the ownership of the property automatically passes over to the remaining joint tenants. It does not need to be passed under the law of succession and it will take precedent over any express wishes left in the deceased party's Will. **Practice example 9.2** highlights this.

Practice example 9.2

Leyton and Adam own their property as joint tenants in law and equity. Adam has a Will which specifically states that he wants his 'share' in any property that he owns at the time of his death to pass to his nephew, Michael. Adam has suddenly passed away and Michael is trying to claim a share in the property that Adam owned with Leyton. Is Michael able to make a claim under the Will?

No, he isn't. The Will does not take precedent over the doctrine of the right of survivorship. That specific gift in the Will would be unenforceable against this particular property and Adam's 'share' would remain with Leyton in its entirety.

Revision tip

An issue can arise here where the co-owners both die at the same time, or where there is uncertainty as to when they died. In this situation s 184 Law of Property Act 1925 provides some guidance and the deaths will be presumed in order of seniority of age.

Using the above example, if Leyton and Adam die in circumstances where it is too difficult to determine who dies first, law will assume that the eldest died first. If Leyton is the eldest that means the right of survivorship applies and the whole property 'passes' to Adam. The gifts in Adam's Will can then be taken into account and Michael would inherit the entirety of the property owned by Leyton and Adam as Adam owned the whole 'share' on the death of Leyton.

Tenancy in common

An initial and important point to make is that the legal title of a property can never be owned as a tenancy in common, meaning the doctrine of survivorship will always apply to the legal title. The equitable title, however (the right to the money from the property), can be held as a joint tenancy or a tenancy in common. Here the owners are said to have an 'undivided share' in the property, so they have an individual share and can do what they please with it, whether that be to sell it or leave it as a gift in their Will.

Revision tip

The term 'undivided share' can sometimes cause some confusion, especially as we are saying that the owners each own their own share in the property, indicating that it is divided.

Undivided share ultimately means that whilst the owners each own their own specific share, they cannot point to a piece of the property and claim that part as their own. The property itself remains 'undivided'.

Also, unlike a joint tenancy, there is no requirement for the four unities to be present. The only requirement for a tenancy in common is that the *unity of possession* is present. So, each co-owner must be able to occupy the whole of the property.

Say Leyton and Adam own their property under a tenancy in common, with both of them 'owning' a 50% share each in the property. They can both occupy the whole of the property satisfying the unity of possession requirement. Adam has drawn up a Will specifying that his share in any property owned by him at the date of his death shall be left in equal shares to his two nephews, Kenny and Austin. **Figure 9.1** illustrates what would happen to the legal and equitable ownership on the death of Adam.

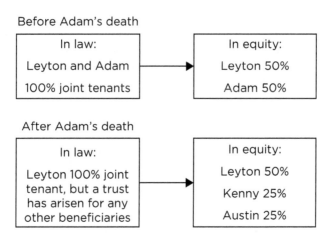

Figure 9.1: Understanding survivorship in a tenancy in common

In this type of situation law imposes a *trust* situation upon Leyton, and he would be considered the *trustee* and Kenny and Austin the *beneficiaries* under the trust. Whilst Leyton is the only person now legally entitled to sell the property, when he does, he has a legal obligation to ensure the beneficiaries under the trust, Kenny and Austin, receive their equitable interest in the property.

The reason for this is simple, it is to avoid situations occurring where there could potentially be numerous tenants in common of both the legal and the equitable title, which could prove very difficult in getting agreement on a sale or having legal documents signed to sell the property. As such, s 34 LPA 1925 prohibited the creation of any tenancy in common of the legal estate and, under the Land Registration Act 2002, a maximum of four people can be registered as the legal title owners. Any greater than four legal owners would mean the four named on the title deeds hold the property on trust for themselves and any additional owners as joint tenants in equity.

Now that we are clear on why the legal ownership of a property cannot be severed, we shall consider how to sever the equitable title of a joint tenancy.

Severance of joint tenancies

Firstly, we will consider the different ways in which severance of joint tenancies can occur, we will then consider the ways in which this can change the equitable ownership of property.

There are five ways in which the equitable ownership can be severed. Those are:

a) by written notice
b) by operating on a party's own share
c) by mutual agreement
d) by mutual conduct
e) forfeiture following unlawful killing.

We shall consider these in turn.

By written notice

This is one of the unilateral methods of severance and also one of the most commonly used. It is a statutory severance and it has the advantage of being very straightforward to carry out. Both statute and case law have established certain requirements for written notice to be effective:

• it must be in writing
• the intention to sever must be immediate
• there must be evidence that it has been delivered.

An important point to note is that the notice does not need to be read by the other co-owner; providing the above conditions are met the severance will be effective. **Practice example 9.4** explains this further.

Practice example 9.4

A husband and wife owned a property under a joint tenancy. Their marriage broke down and the wife posted a notice of severance to her husband by first class post. The following day, and before the letter was delivered, the husband suffered a heart attack. He didn't see the letter and the wife subsequently destroyed it. The husband unfortunately died at a later date. Has effective severance taken place?

Yes, these are the facts of *Kinch v Bullard* [1998] in which the court held the delivery of the letter was sufficient and the husband did not need to actually see it for severance to take effect.

Joint tenant operating on her own share

Initially this may seem incorrect as of course in a joint tenancy there are no individual 'shares'. However, what this actually means is that one of the co-owners has done something that indicates that they do wish to have an individual share.

This could be as simple as one of the co-owners selling or giving away their equitable interest in the property. If they do so, this will sever their equitable interest only; the legal interest will remain exactly the same as that cannot be severed and all other co-owners will remain under the joint tenancy.

Severance would also operate in this way should a co-owner mortgage their equitable interest (we considered equitable mortgages in **Chapter 8**) or it would arise should one of the co-owners become bankrupt. **Figure 9.2** explains how this would work in practice.

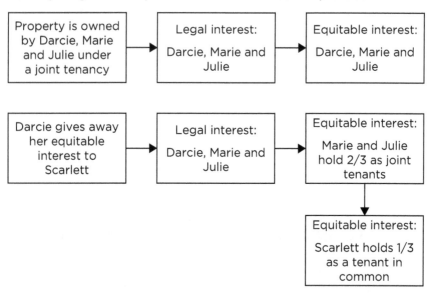

Figure 9.2: Severance by 'operating on her own share'

By mutual agreement

In contrast to the previous two methods, this requires a collective agreement, rather than a unilateral one. So, all equitable joint tenants must agree to sever, although this doesn't need to be in writing – it can be express or implied. Consider **Practice example 9.5** if faced with a question of this type.

Practice example 9.5

Two friends, Luke and Clara, purchased a house together as joint tenants in law and equity. Their friendship broke down and they started discussions over selling Clara's share in the property to Luke.

A price was agreed but then Clara demanded a higher price. Luke unfortunately died before negotiations were concluded. Have their discussions shown a mutual agreement to sever their joint tenancy?

These are the facts of *Burgess v Rawnsley* [1975] in which the court held that even though a final agreement had not been reached, the initial agreement to sell was a sufficient indication of the parties' intention to sever by mutual agreement.

This does demonstrate that there can be some degree of overlap between the different severance methods.

By mutual conduct

As with the previous method, this requires a collective agreement between all co-owners. This will clearly be dependent upon the facts of the case; however, the courts have been clear that inconclusive negotiations to sell one co-owner's share and physical division of land will not amount to severance unless there is a very clear indication of both parties that this is intended.

Forfeiture following unlawful killing

As we know, in a joint tenancy, upon the death of one co-owner the ownership of the legal and equitable estate will fully vest in the other co-owners. As such, on public policy grounds a co-owner who has unlawfully killed another co-owner should not benefit financially from that.

Exam warning

If you do receive a question of this type in the exam then you must remember that the severance will only affect the equitable share of the co-owner who has severed the joint tenancy (unless by mutual agreement or conduct of course). **Figure 9.1** gave an example of this.

Solving disputes between co-owners under TOLATA 1996

You saw in **Figure 9.1** how a trust of land may arise, which is also considered in **Chapter 1** and **Chapter 2**.

The Trusts of Land and Appointment of Trustees Act (TOLATA) 1996 provides a mechanism which can be used by both trustees (eg, people who hold a legal interest in the property) and beneficiaries (eg, people who hold an equitable interest in the land), should there be a dispute over the **trust of land**. It is important to note that the trustees and the beneficiaries can be the same people, an example of this was provided in **Chapter 1**, but we can recap on that briefly here; James and Nicola are the registered title holders and so own the legal title to the property. They made an express declaration when they purchased the property that they would each own a 50% equitable share as tenants in common; as such, they hold the trust property (the legal title) on trust for each other as to 50%.

These types of disputes most commonly arise where one party wishes to sell the trust property but the other party does not. The court will then need to consider a number of factors before making an order for sale.

Key term: trust of land

This is an agreement, either in writing or by actions between the parties, in which the formal legal ownership of the land is separated from the underlying ownership, or the equitable ownership.

The main sections that we shall consider for this book are s 14 and s 15 TOLATA. S 14 provides that anyone with an *interest* in the property is able to make an application to the court to resolve a dispute. Those with an interest are usually other co-owners, mortgagees, trustees or a trustee in bankruptcy of one of the beneficiaries.

S 15 then provides the court with a list of factors they should take into consideration when dealing with the application. Those are:

- s 15(1)(a): the intentions of the person(s) who created the trust. This will be the legal and equitable owners of the land and, as mentioned above, the trust may either be in a written deed or it can be inferred through the action of those parties. If there is no written deed then this intention will be a matter of interpretation by the courts to infer. There is usually always some overlap between this factor and the purpose for which the property is held on trust.
- s 15(1)(b): the purposes for which the property subject to the trust is held. In many cases this is usually as a family home, but the courts will consider the purpose at the time the application is made to the court, which may have changed from the original intentions of the parties who created the trust. **Practice example 9.6** explains this further.

Practice example 9.6

Four friends purchase a piece of land close to the seafront. The intention between them all was to keep the land free from any building or structure as that may have caused the value of their own properties to decrease. They all agreed that they would only sell the land if the majority of them agreed to do so. A dispute over selling the land arose between the four friends. What weight would the court give to the original intentions of the parties?

These are the facts of *Re Buchanan-Wollaston's Conveyance* [1939] and the court looked at the original purpose of buying the land. The purpose was clear and it would not order the sale of the property as the majority of the owners were not in favour of doing so.

- s 15(1)(c): the welfare of any minor who occupies or might reasonably be expected to occupy the property. The court may consider postponing any order of sale if there are children living in the property. The ages of the children are likely to be taken into account and older children are likely to have little weight in the consideration of this factor. This can also be extended to grandchildren living with their grandparents.
- s 15(1)(d): the interests of any secured creditor of any beneficiary. As discussed in **Chapter 8**, if an owner of the property falls behind with the mortgage repayment, the mortgagee may make an application to the court to order a sale.

Revision tip

As there is no priority given to these factors, each case will be considered on its own merits and so careful consideration of the facts in any question is needed to ensure you can correctly identify which remedies are available to the client.

As a final point, it is also worth noting that co-owners can also change their ownership from a tenancy in common to a joint tenancy, but this requires an application to be made to HM Land Registry and that process is outside the scope of this book.

■ KEY POINT CHECKLIST

This chapter has covered the following key knowledge points. You can use these to structure your revision around, making sure to recall the key details for each point, as covered in this chapter.

- You will need to ensure you can identify whether you are dealing with a tenancy in common or joint tenants.
  - Joint tenants mean both the legal and the equitable title in the property are owned collectively as a whole by all owners.
  - There are two distinguishing features of a joint tenancy – the four unities and the right of survivorship.
  - The four unities are possession, interest, title and time. If one or more of these are not present in the legal arrangement then there cannot be a joint tenancy and the ownership will be a tenancy in common. Even if all four unities are present, the ownership will also be a tenancy in common if there is an express declaration confirming this.
- A joint tenancy can be severed in five ways: by written notice, by operating on the party's own share, by mutual agreement, by mutual conduct and by forfeiture from unlawful killing.
  - Remember, if a joint tenancy is severed it destroys the right of survivorship and upon the death of one owner the property will be inherited by whomever the deceased party has left it to in their Will. If there is no Will then the rules of intestacy will apply. It will not automatically transfer to the other co-owner, which does happen with a joint tenancy.
  - A tenancy in common means the legal title only is owned collectively as a whole by all owners but the equitable title (the money) can be owned in equal or unequal shares.
  - Only the equitable title (ie, the money) can be held in unequal shares – the legal title can never be held in this way.
  - Disputes between co-owners can be dealt with by the court under TOLATA 1996. If required to hear a case the court will consider the following factors: intention between the parties, the purpose that the property was purchased for, the welfare of any minors and whether there are any creditors.

■ KEY TERMS AND CONCEPTS

- joint tenancy (**page 215**)
- tenancy in common (**page 215**)
- legal title (**page 216**)
- equitable title (**page 216**)
- trust of land (**page 224**)

■ SQE1-STYLE QUESTIONS

QUESTION 1

A client has sought advice on the legal ownership of a property that she has inherited. Her grandmother left a property to the client and her three cousins. The youngest cousin wants to sell the property immediately and is claiming that he does not need the client's consent to sell as they own it as tenants in common. The client believed they owned the property as joint tenants as they were all left the property at the same time in the grandmother's Will. The client and two other cousins have been registered legal owners for a year, but they held the property on trust for the youngest cousin as he was too young to be registered on the legal title. The client's cousin has recently turned 18 and so has now been registered on the legal title, and he is now saying that he wants the property sold immediately.

Which of the following is the most accurate statement of the legal position in this case?

A. The client is correct – there is clearly unity of possession, interest, title and time here and so the property would be owned as a joint tenancy.

B. The client is correct – there is unity of possession, interest and title, which is all that is needed to demonstrate a joint tenancy is established.

C. As the cousins have all acquired their interest at different times, being when they each reached the age of 18, there is no unity of title and so a tenancy in common will be established.

D. Unless they have all signed an express declaration that they wish to own the property as joint tenants, there will be a tenancy in common.

E. As the cousins have all acquired their interest at different times, being when they each reached the age of 18, there is no unity of time and so a tenancy in common will be established.

QUESTION 2

A client owns a property as joint tenants in law and equity with her partner. The client wishes to sever the joint tenancy and posts a letter by recorded delivery to her partner at their home address. The letter is delivered the next day and the client signs for it. The client died soon afterwards and her partner claims to have never seen the letter. Her partner would like to know if the joint tenancy has been severed.

Which of the following best represents the legal position?

A. The joint tenancy in equity has not been severed. The partner must have seen the letter for this to be a valid severance.

B. The joint tenancy in equity has not been severed, but the joint tenancy in law has. The partner does not need to see the letter for legal tenancy to be valid.

C. The client satisfied all requirements for an effective severance by writing. The partner does not need to see the notice, but it must be posted. The fact it was sent recorded delivery will be sufficient evidence of this.

D. Unless the partner murdered the client, the equitable joint tenancy will never be severed. Forfeiture is the only method that would sever a joint tenancy.

E. This is clear evidence of mutual conduct to sever the equitable joint tenancy and so the severance will be valid.

QUESTION 3

Three clients own their property as joint tenants in law and equity. Client One has a Will which states that her share in any property that she owns at the time of her death will be gifted to her two children. A solicitor has been contacted by one of the children as their mother, Client One, has recently died and the child wants the property to be transferred to her and her brother in accordance with the Will. Clients Two and Three are refusing to discuss this with her.

Which of the following best reflects the legal position in this case?

A. There is a clear tenancy in common of Client One's share as she has acted on her own share by gifting the property in her Will to her children. The children must be added to the title deeds as legal owners.

B. The rules of survivorship apply in a joint tenancy and as such, upon the death of Client One, her legal and equitable share in the property will automatically vest in Clients Two and Three. Client One's children will not be entitled to a share of the property.

C. There is a tenancy in common here and whilst the children will not be placed on the title deeds, they are now beneficiaries under a trust and Clients Two and Three have a legal obligation to ensure the children receive their equitable interest when the property is sold.

D. Whilst the rules of survivorship apply in a joint tenancy, only the legal interest will vest in Clients Two and Three. Client One's equitable interest will pass to her children and they will receive a one-quarter share each.

E. The rules of survivorship apply in a joint tenancy and as such, upon the death of Client One, her legal and equitable share in the property will automatically vest in Clients Two and Three. Client One's children will still be entitled to a share of the property but not until it is sold.

QUESTION 4

Four friends purchase a piece of land near the seafront close to where they live. The purpose was to ensure that this particular piece of land was never developed which would possibly diminish the value of their own homes. The four friends agreed only to sell the land if the majority of them agreed. Client One wishes to sell but the other three all refuse. Client One makes an application to the court under s 14 Trusts of Land and Appointment of Trustees Act (TOLATA) 1996.

Which factors under s 15 TOLATA 1996 is the court most likely to take into consideration?

A. The court will only consider the relevance of any secured creditors and it is their main propriety to ensure any mortgage is repaid.

B. The court will only consider the welfare of any minors who can be expected to occupy the property and as this is a piece of land, with no property built upon it, they will order a sale.

C. The court will only consider the original intention of the parties, and if that intention has changed the court must order a sale of the property.

D. The court will consider any of the factors but will not order a sale of the property unless one of the owners is bankrupt.

E. The court will consider the current purpose of the trust land and the original intention of the parties. If it is clear that the purpose is clear and continuing, then the court will not order a sale.

QUESTION 5

A couple own a property together as joint tenants in law and equity. They have a daughter together who is 18 years old. The couple's relationship breaks down and Client One moves out of the property with their daughter. Some months later Client Two writes to Client One stating that he 'wishes to sever the joint tenancy with immediate effect'. Client Two immediately regrets this decision and breaks into Client one's new home and destroys the letter before Client One can see it. Client Two unfortunately dies two weeks later and his brother contacts Client One to state that he has been left his brother's half share in the property in the Will. The brother wishes to sell the property to release his share but Client One is refusing.

Which of the following best reflects the correct legal advice?

A. The brother does have a legal right over the property as a beneficiary under a trust, and could ask the court to order a sale. It would appear that the original intention of the parties is no longer subsisting, and the court may force a sale.

B. The brother does have a legal right over the property as a beneficiary under a trust, but the court must firstly give consideration to any creditors. If they do not wish to sell the property, then the court will not force a sale.

C. The brother does not have any legal right over the property as the rule of survivorship will apply here as the tenancy was not correctly severed. Clients One and Two were still joint tenants in equity and law and the full property will transfer to Client One on the death of Client Two.

D. The brother does not have any legal right over the property as even though the joint tenancy was effectively severed, Client Two's share of the property will automatically transfer to his daughter.

E. The brother does have a legal right over the property as a beneficiary under a trust, and whilst the original intention of the parties may still be subsisting, the court will also take into account the welfare of any minors. As there is a child who is entitled to live in the property the court will not force a sale.

■ ANSWERS TO QUESTIONS

Answers to 'What do you know already?' questions at the start of the chapter

1) The correct answer was false. A joint tenancy requires the unity of possession, unity of interest, unity of title and unity of time. If one of

those is missing, then unless there is an express declaration to the contrary, the property will be held as a tenancy in common.

2) The correct answer was D. Whilst B could also be correct as there can be collective ownership of the legal and equitable title, the key point here is that the equitable title *can* be held in unequal shares, which is what distinguishes this from a joint tenancy.

3) The correct answer was B. If you are joint tenants in equity and law then each owner collectively owns the property and there is no division of shares, even where one party has contributed more to the purchase than the other. The issue of unequal contributions would usually arise in situations where the legal title is held in the name of one of the parties only and there could be an implied trust, such as constructive trust in that situation.

4) The correct answer was A. As they own the property as tenants in common, the rule of survivorship does not apply. If Abbie does not have a Will then her share will pass under the rules of intestacy. Wilson has a duty, as trustee of her share, to hold the trust money or property until a beneficiary is identified. This means he can sell the property if he wishes, but he must keep her 20% share separate to be paid to the beneficiary.

5) The correct answer was false. There are a number of considerations the court will take into account before reaching a decision. These could be intention of the parties, the purpose for which the property was purchased, the welfare of any minors or the interests of any secured creditors. But the court's powers are not limited to these, and they will take into account any reasonable circumstances of the case.

Answers to end-of-chapter SQE1-style questions

Question 1:

The correct answer was E. This is because for a joint tenancy to be established there must be unity of possession, interest, title and time, which is why option B is incorrect as 'time' is missing. A is incorrect as there is no unity of time here as the cousins all obtained their legal interest in the property when they turned 18, and unless they were all born on the same day then legal title will have been obtained on different days. C is incorrect as they do have unity of title, which occurs when they are all be registered on the title deeds once the youngest cousin has turned 18. D is incorrect as a tenancy in common does not only arise by way of an express declaration and it can also be implied by the actions of the parties.

Question 2:

The correct answer was C. This is because the rules on severance of the equitable title are very clear – all that is required is that it must be made in writing and it also needs to be posted, which is why option A is incorrect. Recorded delivery will be clear evidence that the letter has been posted and the partner does not need to see the letter for this to be valid. B is incorrect as a severance will only ever sever the equitable title and the legal title cannot be severed. D is incorrect as there are other ways, apart from forfeiture, that will sever a joint tenancy. There is no evidence of mutual conduct here and so option E can be disregarded.

Question 3:

The correct answer was B. Options A and C are incorrect as they both mention a tenancy in common, whereas the question explicitly states this is a joint tenancy in law and equity. D and E are incorrect as with a joint tenancy, on the death of one owner the legal and equitable interest will vest automatically with any other remaining joint tenants.

Question 4:

The correct answer was E. This is because the court will look at a number of factors such as intention between the parties, the purpose that the property was purchased for, the welfare of any minors and whether there are any creditors who have an interest in the land. It is clear here that the original purpose of purchasing the land is still continuing. The four friends all agreed that they would only sell if the majority of them agreed to it. This has not changed and so the court would not order a sale. This is why options A, B, C and D are all incorrect as they only focus on one or two specific elements that the court *will* look at, but the court could look at a large number of different factors in determining a case and it is not limited to just one or two specific factors.

Question 5:

The correct answer was A. This is because it is clear here that the joint tenancy has been severed. The letter was posted and it does not matter that it has not been seen by the other person. This means that the rule of survivorship does not apply, which is why option C is incorrect. B is incorrect as the rights of any creditors is not the most important factor for the court to consider. Option D is incorrect as, even though Client Two has a daughter, he has made clear provisions in his Will for his share in the property to pass to his brother; this express declaration takes precedent over other family members who may have been entitled to inherit the asset. Option E is incorrect as Client One moved out with the daughter and so it is no longer meeting that intention. The welfare of a minor will not be a factor as the child of the parties is now an adult.

■ KEY CASES, RULES, STATUTES AND INSTRUMENTS

The SQE1 Assessment Specification requires you to know Trusts of Land and Appointment of Trustees Act 1996 (ss 14 and 15). Candidates might also find it useful to become familiar with these statutes:

Law of Property Act 1925

Land Registration Act 2002.

Index

Lightning Source UK Ltd.
Milton Keynes UK
UKHW020111030222
398095UK00008B/100